THE WORLD TRAVEL MARKET

ROBERT SENIOR

Facts On File Publications
460 Park Avenue South
New York, N.Y. 10016

The World Travel Market

Copyright © 1982 Euromonitor Publications Limited

This edition published 1983

Library of Congress Cataloging in Publication Data

Senior, Robert.
   World travel market

   Includes index.
      1. Tourist trade.   2. Travel.   I. Title.
   G155.A1S435   1983   380.1′459104   82-18314
   ISBN 0-87196-124-5

Printed and bound in Great Britain

THE WORLD TRAVEL MARKET

FOREWORD

This, the latest in Euromonitor's series of FACTFINDER books, examines the international travel market and its growth and development over the last decade. It aims to provide users with an understanding of some of the main trends in international tourist demand and to provide statistical information on tourist consumption in countries throughout the world. In addition, we hope it will provide a useful sourcebook and a guide to further reading.

No single book could hope to cover all aspects of a market as large as international travel, and this book is primarily designed as an introduction to the subject. It also attempts, by the wide use of estimates, to present a truer picture of international tourist demand than some that may have gone before.

Whilst every effort has been made to ensure the accuracy of the contents of this book, the publishers cannot accept responsibility for errors or omissions which may have occurred. All opinions are those of the author.

Robert Senior is Director of Research at Euromonitor.

CONTENTS

LIST OF TABLES

List of Tables — continued

List of Tables — continued

List of Tables — continued

CHARTS

CHAPTER ONE
WORLD TOURISM — An Introduction

Speaking at the California International Travel Mart in 1980, Dr. David Edgell, assistant to the Secretary of Commerce in Washington said, "Tourism is a massive collection of loosely affiliated groups including transportation companies, accommodation concerns, resorts, agents and operators. The magnitude of international tourism worldwide is not always realised . . . . . by any measure, it is both a major and growth industry."

That tourism is a major world industry is beyond dispute; with a turnover in excess of $100 billion dollars, it accounts for 5% of world trade and 1% of the world's gross domestic product. The concerns which directly or indirectly depend on tourism employ thousands of people; they include airlines, shipping firms, hotel chains, finance companies, tour operators, travel agents, car rental firms, caterers, retail establishments and even governments. This book attempts to describe and quantify this major international industry; provide a basis for further research; and discuss some of the broad themes which have run through the world tourist market over the last decade.

Superficially, it is easy to view tourism as a valuable international activity. It brings people together and provides pleasure and relaxation to millions; it opens up the world to its inhabitants, broadening social and cultural horizons; and it also offers one means by which the income of more affluent countries may be redistributed to developing and economically weaker countries. But although there are elements of truth in these points, one can be easily mislead into viewing tourism as a comprehensively good thing; there are adverse factors, too, to consider and take into account. In this introductory section, I want to consider some of the broader issues related to international travel.

Some of the main advantages and disadvantages of international tourism were summarised in a report published by the United Nations Environment Programme in 1979, pictured in a diagram entitled "Costs and Benefits of Tourism", which is reproduced over the page.

The U.N.'s first point is that tourism is advantageous to a country because it provides income and jobs. It also, of course, is an "invisible" export which brings money into a country as tangibly as if a commodity was being sold overseas. It creates industry within the country in the provision of accommodation facilities and other services which tourists require. And it may help to develop communications between the country and others in the form of air transport and other transportation services.

It is not, however, valid to suggest that the flow of currency from developed to developing countries has some international economic virtue. Although many countries place great emphasis on tourism in their development plans, it must be remembered that

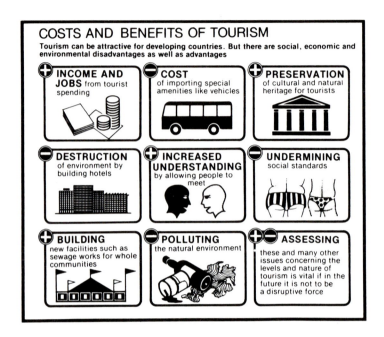

COSTS AND BENEFITS OF TOURISM

Tourism can be attractive for developing countries. But there are social, economic and environmental disadvantages as well as advantages

⊕ **INCOME AND JOBS** from tourist spending

⊖ **COST** of importing special amenities like vehicles

⊕ **PRESERVATION** of cultural and natural heritage for tourists

⊖ **DESTRUCTION** of environment by building hotels

⊕ **INCREASED UNDERSTANDING** by allowing people to meet

⊖ **UNDERMINING** social standards

⊕ **BUILDING** new facilities such as sewage works for whole communities

⊖ **POLLUTING** the natural environment

⊕⊖ **ASSESSING** these and many other issues concerning the levels and nature of tourism is vital if in the future it is not to be a disruptive force

tourism is a product of affluence, and developing countries which do develop their tourist industries are often those which are economically strong and expanding, or small countries or islands whose economic benefits from tourism have little international impact.

Also it must be remembered that many countries who derive financial benefits from tourism are themselves the more prosperous and developed economies of the West, including Western European countries and North America, and the proportion of total world revenue going to South America, Africa or the Far East is relatively small.

The problem for the least developed countries is that they lack the resources to develop their tourist industries. They may be politically unstable, which will deter the holiday tourist, and because they are economically weak, there is limited business interest. So only countries which are growing economically, possess strong reserves, have a high level of foreign investment and sound industry are in a position to finance tourist development and provide the kind of facilities which the tourists demand.

There are clear dangers, too, in overestimating the economic contribution which tourism will bring. As we shall discuss in Chapter Two, there are many reasons why conditions in particular countries may deter the potential tourist market, which is extremely selective. The Caribbean, for example, has discovered that over-reliance on tourism can cause serious economic problems if demand falls away.

So although tourism can have considerable economic advantages if well planned and controlled, it can create problems, too, and only a small proportion of the international tourist spend reaches countries with a real need.

The second observation in the U.N. report is a negative one; also related to cost. The provision of tourist facilities may involve the importation of goods and facilities which are not available in the country. In addition to vehicles, this would also refer to luxury goods, for which there may be little demand in the country. So the provision of tourist facilities may require considerable capital investment.

Added to this, we might also consider the extent to which private enterprises may benefit from the development of a tourist industry, in the form of hotel chains, tour operators, building contractors and airlines. In more affluent countries, this is beneficial to the country concerned in that such amenities will be provided by concerns within the industrial infrastructure. But if countries lack the skills and industrial base to supply such facilities, overseas firms will be used. So much of the financial benefit of tourism may be hived off to private enterprises in other countries.

The third point in the report is that an expansion in the tourist industry will help to preserve cultural and social values, including historical places of interest. Certainly the latter may be true, but I feel that cultural values may in fact suffer from tourism rather than be enhanced. The problem with tourism is that it is a commercial activity first and foremost, and being of a transitory nature, rarely fosters a real understanding of culture and social mores. It is a series of "snapshots" of a country.

This is a particular danger for developing countries where a brief glance at the inhabitants of wealthier countries may disturb the country's social and cultural development. A superficial veneer of this sort offers few long-term benefits for the country as a whole.

The fourth point made by the U.N. refers to the destruction of the environment by building hotels and accommodation facilities. This in itself is probably not a major problem if planned and controlled, but of more potential harm is the development of tourist sections in towns crammed with hotels, bars, restaurants, cinemas and nightclubs catering for the tourist demand.

Tourist development inevitably has a snowball effect which can easily get out of control, and can change the physical and social face of a country or city.

Taking the fifth point by the U.N., I would not deny that international contact must have beneficial consequences for the world as a whole by as the U.N. puts it, "allowing people to meet". Of course, this can also have adverse results; tourists carry wealth, and can escalate the crime rate, or produce antagonism among the national population. It can result in morally suspect activities. But tourists who do take a real interest in the countries they meet can develop awareness and understanding, and certainly tourism can help multi-racial relations. Added to this, the business travel market can help to broaden and develop the role of world trade.

I have touched on the U.N.'s sixth point, that tourism can undermine social values, in considering the potential influence on a country's culture. Certainly a country which becomes the focus of mass market appeal can radically alter in character and image, and some countries take steps to avoid this occurring. Generally, it depends on the type of tourists, and where they travel to; tourism might equally enhance social standards in some circumstances.

The penultimate point made in the U.N. document is that a development of the tourist industry will result in the provision of facilities which will benefit the country as a whole. This is a valid point, and perhaps the best example of this is the building of major sporting stadiums for international events which can then be used by the inhabitants of the country.

The final comment by the U.N. is that tourism can result in the pollution of the natural environment, again a valid point.

The U.N.'s comment that assessment of the problems of tourism is vital to avoid disruption is an important one. Tourism can have considerable benefits and advantages to countries, regions as the world as a whole, but it can create problems as well. Above all, it should be remembered that it is an industry like any other, with at its base the commodity of travelling people. It is a product of affluence, and it is the affluent countries who most benefit from its usage and its demand.

4

CHAPTER TWO
KEY ASPECTS OF WORLD TRAVEL

Before looking in detail at the individual components which make up the world travel market, I want to begin by considering some of the central issues which affect and influence the structure of world demand for tourist services. Such influences take many forms; they may be political, economic, social, geographical or cultural, but they all have a bearing on the trends in international tourism and the direction of international tourist flows.

I want to begin by distinguishing the main types of tourism, although these are dealt with more fully in Chapter Seven. The distinctions are important because the reasons why a person is a tourist affects choice of destination.

Two types of tourists have fairly fixed reasons for their choice of destination. Firstly, there are tourists who visit friends and relatives, where the locations are self-evident. Secondly, there are business tourists whose destinations will be determined by the trading partner concerned. But in the case of the leisure/holiday tourist, who make up a large proportion of the total world tourism market, various factors can encourage or discourage the potential tourist market. In this chapter, I want to consider some of these factors, and the extent to which they have influenced tourist demand in some of the main tourist countries of the world.

Central to the whole tourist market is the question of cost. Over the last two years, there has been a growing concern over the cost of travel because of the world recession, and there are several ways in which costs can be affected.

The most obvious is in fluctuations of the **exchange rate**. This is a fairly recent phenomenon, sparked off by the rise in energy costs in the early 1970's. Since then, the strength of currency in relation to the currencies of other countries can seriously affect the level of tourist consumption.

The most obvious recent example of this has been the devaluation of the U.S. dollar in 1980, which made most European currencies strong in comparison. This made the U.S.A. an extremely attractive destination for Europeans, whilst having the opposite effect on Americans coming to Europe. As a result, we saw a massive increase in the number of Europeans travelling to the States.

As tourism is an "invisible" export, fluctuations in the exchange rate have an opposite effect on tourism as they do on exports of goods and services. So U.K. tourists visiting the U.S.A. benefited from the strong pound, while British industry suffered.

Just as a weak exchange rate is an encouragement to tourist consumption, a rising **rate of inflation** is a deterrent. Many countries, notably in Western Europe and

South America, have suffered from having a high rate of inflation — in the former region, two of the chief examples are Spain and Italy. In South America, virtually all countries have a high rate of inflation which make them expensive to visit.

The best example of this is Mexico, which was for a long time a cheap place to visit. Over the last two years, Mexico's rate of inflation has made it one of the most expensive places in The Americas, with prices 20% up on the U.S.A. The solution is to protect the tourist industry against inflation by special financial arrangements, as Israel has done.

Another central cost aspect is the cost of transportation, and here we have to consider the whole concept of **low-cost travel**. This has been most significantly apparent in the airline industry, where air fares on the North American and Far Eastern routes have fallen sharply. This not only affects the number of tourists but also the types of tourists and the types of tourist trips, and the exodus to the U.S.A. in the late 70's from Europe mirrors the travel boom to Spain in the 60's.

The future development of low-cost travel may now be affected by the collapse of Laker Airways in the United Kingdom, resulting in a stabilisation in the fare price war. But certainly a country's tourist intake can be dramatically increased if the organised sector of the travel industry develops package tours to that location.

In fact, the provision of such facilities may not be merely linked to low air fares. The trend is for tour operators to offer organised tourist trips to increasingly adventurous locations, some at quite considerable expense. So the **development of organised travel** is in general an encouraging factor.

Various physical and geographical factors can influence the tourist market. In Chapter Six of this book, I discuss the direction of travel, and note that it is partly guided by **geographical proximity**, and **cultural, historical and political affiliations.** Many tourists travel to their neighbouring countries, or to countries in the same region. Inhabitants of countries with ex-colonies often visit them; many East Europeans go to Cuba. In addition, **climatic conditions** can deter tourists; in 1981, Switzerland and Austria suffered from bad weather.

At a more extreme end, **natural disasters** are a major problem for the tourist industry. Tourist intake in Italy suffered following the earthquakes in 1981, while in Jamaica, "Hurricane Allen" destroyed the tourist infrastructure in 1980.

Political conditions are also important. Tourists will not favour countries which are politically unstable — they want no sense of unease on a tourist trip, especially if it is a leisure trip. There are many obvious examples of this, such as Iran, Afghanistan, El Salvador and Poland, but there are others which are more surprising, such as the failed coup in the tranquil Seychelles in 1981. Whether fears of political disturbance are justified or not, they are certainly an important element in the choice of a tourist destination.

Like political instability, **incidence of crime** and **terrorist activities** such as bombings can have a serious effect on the tourist market, particularly if a particular case catches the eye of the international press. There have been many recent examples of crime rates hitting tourist demand; muggings in Miami have detracted from the state's rising popularity among the British, while another U.S. state, Hawaii, has a rising crime rate which belies its image as a tranquil and idyllic resort and resurrects images of Hawaii-based crime series.

Terrorist activities have hit many tourist markets. The most obvious example is Northern Ireland, where visits from or through the UK fell by half between 1967 and 1978. Another, the ETA bombing campaigns in Spain in 1979 and 1980, particularly as some of these were directed at tourist hotels. Basically, tourists do not want to feel under threat when they visit a country, whether it be from natural disaster, political instability or violence.

Perhaps the most complete example of all three hitting a market has been Jamaica; apart from the hurricanes, the country experienced daily violence in the streets during the political resurgence in 1980, and a general escalation in the crime rate. Jamaica's popularity as a tourist market has slumped, and the new government under Eddie Seaga is now actively engaged in restoring the tourist industry and the country's popularity as a tourist destination.

Generally speaking, one would assume that the unpopularity of a political regime, or the policies it pursues, would hit the tourist industry, but this does not always seem to be the case. International tourism is an individual matter, and left free to individuals to decide where they choose to visit, and many individuals seem happy to disassociate their tourist trips with political issues, unless of course, there is a real threat of violence. South Africa, for example, seems to be doing very well out of tourism, yet in many ways it is isolated. SATOUR's London Manager describes tourism as a "grown-up fairy tale".

Many decisions about tourist travel are related to **image**, and there is always a demand to go somewhere further, more exciting, more exotic. Various types of tourism produce different images, and the countries themselves often seek, through their advertising to promote a particular concept, whether mass market; upmarket; youth-orientated; adventurous and so forth.

The search for adventure must have reached its ultimate in the booming demand for tourist trips to the Antarctic, which has been visited by about 10,000 people in the last decade. Despite the high cost — about $10,000 dollars per head for a 40 day cruise, the market is apparently expanding fast.

There are various other reasons why people travel to certain countries, including unusual reasons. The Gambia has apparently done very well out of the publicity it received in Alex Haley's "Roots", and thousands of people have visited Bali under the mistaken book impression that it is connected to Bali Ha'i, made famous by "South Pacific" and the books of James Michener. In general any film, book or television programme which focusses its attention on a particular location can help the tourist market if it presents the country in an attractive light.

To conclude this section, we can summarise the advantages and disadvantages as follows:-

Advantages	Disadvantages
1. Physically attractive	1. High Inflation rate
2. Good climate	2. Strong currency
3. Geographically proximate	3. High crime rate
4. Low-cost travel	4. Incidence of terrorism
5. Good facilities	5. Incidence of natural disasters
6. Politically stable	6. Politically unstable
7. Economically prosperous	7. Unpopular government or regime
8. Cultural, social or historical ties	8. Bad publicity
9. New, exciting location	9. Economically weak
10. Cheap accommodation	10. Well-tried location

CHAPTER THREE
ECONOMICS OF TOURISM

I want in this section to examine the contribution made by tourism to the world economy. We have already noted that this is a big industry, employing thousands of people worldwide; that the economies of some countries almost entirely depend on tourism, and that a wide range of international financial services have developed around the expansion of the world tourist market. In this section, we shall be considering how much is earned in tourist receipts by countries throughout the world; how much is spent by the residents of those countries in overseas travel; and tourism's contribution to gross domestic products and trade. Utilising eight standard regions, we can see the net balances for tourism on a regional basis, and finally gauge the total world market for tourism in value terms.

Firstly, some definitions.

Travel Receipts are the financial receipts of a country in the form of payments for goods and services made by foreign tourists out of foreign currency resources. They should, in theory, exclude international fare payments. This is the definition used by the World Tourism Organisation, and also used by the International Monetary Fund in their "Balance of Payments" publications. They call them "travel credits". Where national statistical offices and tourist offices publish figures, they should correlate with these definitions, although some discrepancies are in evidence.

Travel Expenditure is the opposite of the above; it refers to payments by own residents in foreign countries, again excluding fares. This relates to "travel debits" in the I.M.F. classification.

The I.M.F. "Balance of Payments" undoubtedly offers the most comprehensive summary of travel receipts and expenditure, and has listings not available from national sources. But the figures are rounded, and are presented in "SDR" (Special Drawing Rights) units. So they have to be converted at the rate of exchange, which is given. Also, many of the figures carry notes which point to discrepancies in data collection. So I have used some I.M.F. figures but tried to use national sources as far as possible.

*　　　　　　*　　　　　　*

In 1980, the total world tourism market was worth $105 billion, which is the total value of all tourist receipts, or the total value of expenditure. In theory, the figures should be the same of course, but statistics are rarely to finely tuned.

To form a picture of the overall value of tourism in the world, we can relate tourist receipts and expenditure to the pattern of world trade. Tourist receipts are an "invisible" export, in that they bring money into the country in the same way that exports do. And on the other hand, tourist expenditure is a debit item which can be related to imports. Total world exports in 1980 amounted to $1,856 billion, total world imports — allowing for duties — amounted to $1,936 billion.

In that year, the ratio of total tourist receipts to total exports was 5.7%, while expenditure took a 5.4% share of total imports. But two years earlier, the proportions were higher than this; in 1978, receipts accounted for 6.3% of total world exports, and expenditure, 6.0% of total imports.

In 1981, however the increase in the value of world trade was minimal, and the estimated growth of 14.5% in world tourist receipts will give tourism a 6.4% ratio of total exports — the highest for the full period.

We can see, therefore, that there has been a decline in the ratio between world trade and tourism since the end of 1978, despite the continued growth in international tourist travel, and it is this financial slackening of demand that has troubled the travel industry.

Table 1. The World Tourist Market in Financial Terms 1976-1980

($ million)	Receipts			Expenditure		
	Tourist Receipts	Total Exports	Ratio	Tourist Expenditure	Total Imports	Ratio
1976	49,719	909,400	5.5%	50,023	926,400	5.4%
1977	60,966	1,035,200	5.9%	58,332	1,067,300	5.5%
1978	76,107	1,201,600	6.3%	74,321	1,245,600	6.0%
1979	91,382	1,517,500	6.0%	90,974	1,568,800	5.8%
1980	106,107	1,855,700	5.7%	104,700	1,935,800	5.4%
1981e	121,500	1,900,000	6.4%	120,000	1,980,000	6.1%

Source: Own Calculations based on I.M.F. and various sources
Note: The import and export figures featured above and throughout this chapter do not include tourist receipts and expenditure, they are presented as a comparison as tourist earnings are considered an invisible trade item. The trade figures includes goods, but not services.

Looking at this total market in regional terms, we can see that over 50% of all world tourist receipts are accounted for by the countries of Western Europe, and this dominant region has in fact improved its position since 1976, and more than doubled its tourist receipts.

The second main region to benefit financially from tourism is North and Central America, but the share held by this region has fallen over the last five years from about one-quarter to one-fifth. The main growth in receipts has occurred in the Far East, up from a 5.4% share in 1976 to 7.3% in 1980.

Worldwide, tourist receipts account for 1% of the total gross domestic product.

Turning now to a regional analysis of expenditure, we find that Western Europe again accounts for over 50%, so it virtually puts back into the market what it takes out. Most of the other regions also have levels of expenditure which are compatible with their tourist receipts. The main gainer from tourism in terms of the balance of payments (credits less debits) is Oceania, which had a net balance of $2.5 billion in 1980; this was more than the net balance in Western Europe. The only other region to show a positive balance was North and Central America, with a balance of $1.85 billion. We can see, therefore, that despite the presence of much travelling nations (Canada, U.S.A., Australia) within these regions, the popularity of islands in The Caribbean and The Pacific, and the U.S.A. itself, has been enough to produce a net gain in tourist earnings for the regions as a whole.

Worldwide, tourist expenditure accounts for 1.5% of total consumer expenditure, but almost 5% in North Africa and the Middle East.

Table 2. Tourism Receipts and Expenditure by Region - Balance of Payments 1980

($ million)	Receipts	Expenditure	Balance
Western Europe	59,062	56,807	+ 2,255
Eastern Europe	3,228	1,582	+ 1,646
North and Central America	21,616	19,763	+ 1,853
South America	2,029	3,983	- 3,983
North Africa and Middle East	5,435	9,246	- 3,811
Africa	2,194	2,383	- 189
Far East	7,666	8,587	- 921
Oceania	4,877	2,349	+ 2,528
Total	106,107	104,700	+ 1,407

Source: Own Calculations from I.M.F. / Other sources

World Tourist Receipts by Region 1980
Unit: $ billion

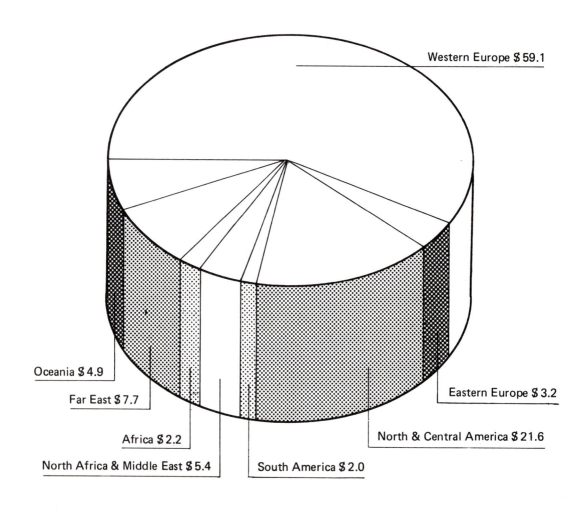

Western Europe $ 59.1

Oceania $ 4.9

Far East $ 7.7

Africa $ 2.2

North Africa & Middle East $ 5.4

South America $ 2.0

Eastern Europe $ 3.2

North & Central America $ 21.6

Total: $ 106.1 billion

Table 3. Tourist Receipts by Region 1976-1980

($ million)	1976	1977	1978	1979	1980
Western Europe	26,606	33,659	42,624	51,442	59,062
Eastern Europe	2,046	2,313	2,880	3,108	3,228
North and Central America	11,917	12,425	15,106	18,026	21,616
South America	957	1,213	1,481	1,721	2,029
North Africa and Middle East	2,846	3,402	3,983	4,944	5,435
Africa	949	1,519	1,594	1,759	2,194
Far East	3,385	4,122	5,299	6,508	7,666
Oceania	2,176	2,313	3,140	3,874	4,877
Total	50,882	60,966	76,107	91,382	106,107

Source: Own Calculations

Table 4. Tourist Expenditure by Region 1976-1980

($ million)	1976	1977	1978	1979	1980
Western Europe	24,935	30,030	38,207	48,952	56,807
Eastern Europe	955	1,109	1,354	1,481	1,582
North and Central America	12,445	2,941	15,266	16,841	19,763
South America	1,823	2,353	3,134	3,540	3,983
North Africa and Middle East	3,620	4,617	6,305	7,723	9,246
Africa	1,496	1,624	1,839	2,022	2,383
Far East	3,314	4,172	6,425	8,324	8,587
Oceania	1,435	1,486	1,791	2,091	2,349
Total	50,023	58,332	74,321	90,974	104,700

Source: Own Calculations

Table 5. Tourist Receipts as a Proportion of Total Gross Domestic Product 1979

	Total GDP	Tourist Receipts	%
Western Europe	3,224,000	51,442	1.6
Eastern Europe	1,055,000	3,108	0.3
North and Central America	2,924,000	18,026	0.6
South America	373,000	1,721	0.6
North Africa and Middle East	360,000	4,944	1.5
Africa	240,000	1,759	0.7
Far East	1,579,000	6,508	0.4
Oceania	147,000	3,874	2.6
Total	9,902,000	91,382	0.9

Source: Own Calculations

Table 6. Tourist Expenditure as a Proportion of Total Consumer Expenditure 1979

($ million)	Total Consumer Expenditure	Tourist Expenditure	%
Western Europe	1,713,200	48,592	2.8
Eastern Europe	744,400	1,481	0.2
North and Central America	1,758,100	16,841	1.0
South America	298,800	3,540	1.2
North Africa and Middle East	159,800	7,723	4.8
Africa	138,900	2,022	1.5
Far East	977,900	8,324	0.9
Oceania	91,900	2,091	2.3
Total	5,883,000	90,614	1.5

Source: Own Calculations

Table 7. Tourist Receipts and Expenditure in OECD Countries 1978-1980

	Share of International Tourist Receipts in Exports of Goods and Services			Share of International Tourist Expenditure in Imports of Goods and Services		
	1978	1979	1980*	1978	1979	1980
Germany	2.8	2.8	2.8	9.2	8.8	8.7
Austria	22.0	20.4	20.4	9.9	9.4	8.2
Belgium-Luxembourg	2.2	2.2	2.0	4.1	3.8	3.4
Denmark	6.6	6.2	5.5	6.0	6.3	5.9
Spain	24.5	21.6	(19.9)	2.5	3.0	(2.6)
Finland	4.2	4.0	3.7	4.0	3.6	3.0
France	5.5	5.0	5.1	4.3	4.0	3.6
Greece	20.6	19.7	20.7	2.7	2.4	2.6
Ireland	5.9	5.4	-	4.2	4.0	-
Iceland	2.1	2.0	1.9	4.7	4.5	4.3
Italy	8.6	8.7	8.5	1.8	1.7	1.6
Norway	3.4	3.0	2.6	6.7	6.2	5.5
Netherlands	2.0	1.6	-	5.3	4.9	-
Portugal	16.4	17.6	16.3	2.7	3.1	2.7
United Kingdom	4.8	4.5	4.2	3.1	3.4	4.1
Sweden	2.7	2.6	2.5	6.1	5.6	5.2
Switzerland	9.0	8.5	-	7.0	6.9	-
Turkey	7.7	8.5	-	1.6	1.6	-
Europe	5.7	5.5	5.5	5.4	5.1	5.0
Canada	3.8	3.8	3.7	6.1	4.8	4.9
United States	3.3	2.9	2.9	3.7	3.3	3.1
North America	3.4	3.1	3.1	4.2	3.6	3.4
Australia	2.6	2.4	2.7	3.4	2.9	2.5
New Zealand	3.6	3.3	3.2	7.3	7.6	7.0
Japan	0.4	0.4	0.4	3.8	3.6	2.7
Australasia-Japan	0.8	0.8	0.8	3.9	3.6	2.9

Source: OECD - Balance of Payment Division
Notes: * Provisional figures   ( ) Estimates

Before looking in more detail at individual regions, I have included an extract from the current OECD report on tourism, which features calculations from the OECD Balance of Payments Division on the proportion of exports and imports of goods and services which are accounted for by tourism. This is more useful than the trade figures published by the United Nations or the International Monetary Fund, which only cover goods, not services.

We can now look at tourist receipts and expenditure within the eight regions.

1.　　Western Europe

We have noted that this region dominates the world market in terms of tourist receipts and expenditure, showing a positive balance between the two of around $2 billion.

The leading country to benefit from tourist receipts in 1980 was Italy, a country which has shown a marked advancement in its earnings from tourism over recent years. As recently as 1976, Italy had only a 10% "share" of the Western European market, behind five other countries.

Second to Italy comes France with a 14% market share. This has held fairly stable over recent years although it dipped slightly in the later 70's. Then four countries — Austria, West Germany, Spain and the United Kingdom — have about 11% each.

Italy has gained at the expense of Spain, Switzerland, the Netherlands and Scandinavia. The other country to show marked growth has been Portugal.

The West Germans dominate tourist expenditure, accounting for over one-third of the total. No other country approaches this level of tourist spending; France and the United Kingdom account for only 11% each. The Netherlands is notable in having a high expenditure level in relation to the size of the population; its share of 8% is not that far short of even the U.K., and well ahead of Italy with its much larger population.

Turning to the net balance of payments, we can see that Germany's extravagance in tourism produces a negative balance of over $14 billion — a staggering sum. And the Netherlands, too, with its limited tourist market but adventurous inhabitants suffers a net inbalance of close to $3 billion. But most of the other countries of Western Europe reap benefits from the tourism industry, notably the key Mediterranean countries; Spain gained $5.7 billion from tourism in 1980, Italy a substantial $7 billion. France and the U.K. are net gainers, too, but whereas France has shown consistent growth in her balance of payments from tourism, the United Kingdom's benefits have fluctuated and the gap has narrowed over the last two years.

16

The most notable contributions made by tourism to the gross domestic product occur in Austria, Cyprus (both 7%) and especially Malta (21%). Average for this region — 1.6% — is higher than the world average, although even developed tourist nations such as Spain and Italy derive only 2-3% of their GDP from this source.

The biggest spenders in proportion to total consumer expenditure are again the inhabitants of a small country — Iceland. They spend 40% of their consumer spending on overseas tourism. No other country approaches this level, or even exceeds 10%; a few such as Austria, Ireland, the Netherlands and Norway exceed 5%.

2.   Eastern Europe

Only 3% of the world tourist revenue is generated in the Eastern bloc countries, but this is sufficient to maintain a healthy balance because expenditure by the inhabitants of these countries is extremely limited. If we look at the region on a country-by-country basis, we can see that its positive balance is almost entirely attributable to the tourist receipts of one country — Yugoslavia, which has a considerable net balance of payments for tourism of $1 billion. Yugoslavia, in fact, accounts for 38% of all tourist receipts in this region, while spending only 11%.

Several countries hold significant shares of the tourist market in Eastern Europe, led by Hungary with 15%. The main spenders are (or were) the Poles, accounting for a quarter of all tourist expenditure.

Comparing tourist receipts with GDP for these countries, we find that the average is an extremely low 0.3%. Even Yugoslavia only derives 2% of her total GDP from tourism, and this is a minute 0.1% in the USSR.

Tourist expenditure as a proportion of consumer expenditure is equally insignificant.

3.   North and Central America

This region derives a substantial income from tourist earnings, and despite the presence of heavy overseas spenders such as the Americans and Canadians, the region has a positive balance of payments. In fact, a fall in the expenditure by U.S. residents overseas over the last year or so has been juxtaposed with the growing popularity of the country as a destination, with the result that the previous deficit of over $1 billion has been virtually eroded.

The U.S.A. does in fact dominate the incomings and outgoings of the region; accounting for 47% of receipts and 53% of expenditure in 1980; in 1976, the same proportions were much further adrift at 58% and 45%. The other major spenders are the

Mexicans and the Canadians, each accounting for about 20% of total expenditure for this region. As most of the other countries in the region are small and mainly tourist-orientated, they account for very small shares of the remaining 6% of the market. And it is interesting to note that their shares of tourist receipts are of almost equal insignificance, mostly under 1%, with only the Bahamas reaching 3%.

The only country in the region to have a net gain between receipts and expenditure in excess of $1 million is Mexico. Most of the Caribbean islands do have positive balances as one would expect, but these are in the region of $100-500 million. This is of course enough to make a sizeable contribution to the Gross Domestic Products of these countries; 55% in The Bahamas, and the British Virgin Isles, over 20% in Barbados, Bermuda, Netherlands Antilles and Trinidad & Tobago. And as a measure of the industrial strength of the U.S.A., we might note that the country's earnings from tourism are a mere 0.4% of total GDP.

4.   South America

This region has the most substantial deficit between tourism receipts and expenditure of all the eight regions, almost $4 billion in 1980. The region is also the lowest earner from tourist receipts, these accounting for only 2% of the world total in 1980.

Virtually all the countries in South America have a trading deficit in tourism terms, but this is substantial in Venezuela, where the net balance was a negative $1.6 billion in 1980. Only one country in the 13 in this region had a significant positive balance; this was Peru, who earned $160 million net in 1980, this having grown from virtually nothing five years earlier.

Venezuela accounted for almost 50% of total tourist expenditure for this region in 1980, well ahead of Brazil at 12.5%. But two countries, Colombia and Argentina took the leading shares of the receipts, both with 17%.

With a regional average of only 0.6%, no country in this region derives more than a small percentage of its GDP from tourism.

5.   North Africa and Middle East

Tourist expenditure by countries in this region substantially exceeds money received, and while both have increased quite rapidly, the increase in spending has been especiallly pronounced, rising from 6% of the world total in 1976 to 9% in 1980.

In terms of tourist receipts, two countries dominate and it is interesting to note that Saudi Arabia's receipts are well in excess of Israel. The former had a one-quarter

18

share of the region's receipts in 1980, while Israel had only 16%. Next in running are primarily tourist locations such as Jordan and Tunisia.

But if Saudi Arabia is a high tourist earner, it is also a heavy spender, accounting for 38% of the region's expenditure in 1980. This resulted in a substantial deficit in the balance of payments of over $2 billion in that year. Whereas the receipts which the country had received from tourism have remained fairly steady, the level of expenditure has shot up over the last five years — it was only 12% of the region's total in 1976. Many other countries have also shown a net deficit, the main exceptions being Tunisia, Israel and Morocco.

Several of the Arab states derive a considerable proportion of their GDP from overseas tourist visits. The highest contribution is in Jordan, at 22%, followed by Bahrain and Tunisia with around 10%. And overseas expenditure also takes a large proportion of the total consumer spending by some of the smaller countries in the region, notably Bahrain (33%) and Kuwait (25%).

6.   Africa

Africa's contribution to the world market is a small one, both in terms of receipts and expenditure. The region also has a negative balance of payments, albeit a marginal one of under $200 million in 1980.

In terms of tourist receipts, three countries stand out well above the rest; they are Egypt, with 35% in 1980, South Africa with 28%, and further down, Kenya with 10%. All the other countries have insignificant shares, all under 4%, most under 1%, of the total tourist receipts in the region.

South Africa is however of equal importance in terms of expenditure, and as a result has a net deficit in her balance of payments. In terms of expenditure, Nigeria becomes much more significant, with a 15% share in 1980, giving her a pronounced inbalance of $300 million, whilst Egypt, spending only 10% of the total for the region, shows a "profit" of over $500 million. A large number of countries in this region spend more than they earn, and it is only Egypt's presence that prevents a substantial negative balance of payments for the region as a whole.

Tourism generally makes a limited contribution to GDP, with the obvious exception of the Seychelles, which derives 40% of its GDP from tourists. Only two countries have more than a 5% level of contribution; Gambia and Swaziland, both with 8%. But tourist expenditure can be a significant destination for consumer expenditure, close to 10% in some countries, where private income is very low.

7.   Far East

This region has shown considerable growth in the income derived from tourist receipts, which accounted for 7.2% of the world's receipts in 1980 against 5.7% in 1976. But because of the presence of one of the major travelling nations — Japan — the region as a whole continues to have an overall deficit in its balance of payments. This has been compounded by the substantial rise in overseas spending by the Japanese over recent years, rising to $4 billion in 1980, from $1.1 billion in 1976. Most countries in the Far East have in fact a positive balance of tourist payments, the only other exceptions out of 25 countries being China and Indonesia.

Tourist receipts are broadly split but three countries stand out above the rest; they are Hong Kong, Singapore and Taiwan. Together, these three countries account for 50% of the total tourist receipts for the area, and being small countries, they all have a healthy trading balance in tourism. Japan accounts for over 50% of all tourist spending by the region, with no other country exceeding 10%.

The contribution of tourist receipts to Gross Domestic Product is high in some countries in this region, again notably the smaller ones. Singapore derives 12.5% of its GDP from this source, and Hong Kong, 7.5%. But the regional average is a low 0.4% due in part to the minimal contribution to Japan in terms of its considerable output. This is further indicated by the expenditure level, with tourist expenditure by the Japanese accounting for under 1% of the total consumer spending in this country, despite its dominance in the region.

8.   Oceania

The Oceania region receives about 5% of total world tourist expenditure, and spend only 2%, so it has a healthy positive balance of payments. This is mainly because of the presence of Hawaii, which is the recipient of two-thirds of all tourist expenditure in the region. With a minimal expenditure level, Hawaii's net balance is a lucrative $3.3 billion, and is rising steadily.

The region contains two well travelled nations, Australia and New Zealand, who both spend considerably more than they earn. But most of the other countries in this region are Pacific Islands which cater for tourists and have small populations, so they show positive balances. Also, in such countries as Fiji, French Polynesia and Vanuatu, the tourist contribution to Gross Domestic Product is high.

Australia and New Zealand dominate expenditure with 75% and 23% respectively, this leaving a meagre 2% for all the rest. Expenditure in Australia accounts for 2% of private consumption expenditure compared with 4% for New Zealand.

Table 8.　　　　　　　　　　**TOURIST RECEIPTS**

Region 1 : Western Europe

($ million)	1976	1977	1978	1979	1980
Andorra	2	2	3	3	3
Austria	3,141	3,755	4,714	5,603	6,470
Belgium*	959	1,163	1,249	1,629	1,810
Cyprus	50	58	89	141	200
Denmark	803	940	1,125	1,312	1,337
Finland	323	355	441	534	683
France	3,613	4,384	5,903	6,826	8,235
Germany, West	3,211	3,972	4,847	5,741	6,640
Gibraltar	4	5	5	5	6
Greece	824	981	1,326	1,663	1,850
Iceland	12	15	19	22	23
Ireland	247	322	414	527	612
Italy	2,526	4,762	6,285	8,185	8,914
Jersey	132	140	150	179	185
Liechtenstein	5	5	5	5	5
Luxembourg	*	*	*	*	*
Malta	67	81	127	213	267
Monaco	15	16	18	20	23
Netherlands	1,061	1,110	1,254	1,325	1,640
Norway	393	485	558	600	742
Portugal	317	405	592	940	1,146
San Marino	1	2	2	2	3
Spain	3,083	4,003	5,488	6,484	6,968
Sweden	303	446	538	638	960
Switzerland	2,191	1,943	2,446	2,568	3,110
Turkey	181	205	230	281	320
United Kingdom	3,144	4,104	4,796	5,996	6,910
TOTAL	26,606	33,659	42,624	51,442	59,062

Source:　IMF/UN/WTO/OECD/National Offices/Own Estimates.

21

Table 9.   **TOURIST EXPENDITURE**

Region 1 : Western Europe

($ million)	1976	1977	1978	1979	1980
Andorra	5	5	5	5	5
Austria	1,518	2,098	2,449	2,966	3,163
Belgium*	1,609	1,889	2,345	2,969	3,272
Cyprus	12	29	37	48	50
Denmark	748	942	1,146	1,542	1,560
Finland	317	355	399	489	593
France	3,421	3,926	4,294	5,191	6,001
Germany, West	8,954	10,979	14,397	17,952	20,827
Gibraltar	-	-	-	-	-
Greece	90	89	142	202	190
Iceland	17	27	33	39	42
Ireland	196	237	353	518	535
Italy	708	894	1,206	1,507	1,907
Jersey	-	-	-	-	-
Liechtenstein	3	3	3	3	3
Luxembourg	*	*	*	*	*
Malta	13	23	26	21	41
Monaco	5	6	6	6	6
Netherlands	1,886	2,454	3,402	4,804	4,637
Norway	633	870	1,061	1,154	1,304
Portugal	140	136	162	245	289
San Marino	-	-	-	-	-
Spain	404	533	567	922	1,229
Sweden	1,058	1,243	1,429	1,750	2,230
Switzerland	1,211	1,114	1,668	2,030	2,357
Turkey	208	269	103	95	115
United Kingdom	1,779	1,909	2,974	4,497	6,454
TOTAL	24,935	30,030	38,207	48,952	56,807

Source: IMF/UN/WTO/OECD/National Offices/Own Estimates.

Table 10.   **BALANCE OF TOURISM PAYMENTS**

Region 1 : Western Europe

($ million)	1976	1977	1978	1979	1980
Andorra	− 3	− 3	− 2	− 2	− 2
Austria	1,623	1,657	2,265	2,637	3,307
Belgium*	− 650	− 726	−1,095	−1,340	−1,462
Cyprus	38	29	52	96	150
Denmark	55	− 2	− 21	− 230	− 223
Finland	6	0	42	45	90
France	192	458	1,609	1,635	2,234
Germany, West	−5,743	−7,007	−9,550	−12,211	−14,187
Gibraltar	4	5	5	5	6
Greece	734	892	1,184	1,461	1,660
Iceland	− 5	− 12	− 14	− 17	− 19
Ireland	51	85	61	9	77
Italy	1,818	3,868	5,079	6,678	7,007
Jersey	132	140	150	179	185
Liechtenstein	2	2	2	2	2
Luxembourg	*	*	*	*	*
Malta	54	58	101	192	226
Monaco	10	10	12	14	17
Netherlands	− 825	−1,344	−2,148	−3,479	−2,997
Norway	− 240	− 385	− 503	− 554	− 562
Portugal	177	269	430	695	857
San Marino	1	2	2	2	3
Spain	2,679	3,470	4,921	5,562	5,739
Sweden	− 755	− 797	− 891	−1,112	1,270
Switzerland	980	829	778	538	753
Turkey	− 27	− 64	127	186	205
United Kingdom	1,365	2,195	1,822	1,499	456
TOTAL	1,671	3,629	4,417	2,490	2,255

Source: IMF/UN/WTO/OECD/National Offices/Own Estimates.

Table 11. TOURIST RECEIPTS AS A PROPORTION OF GROSS DOMESTIC PRODUCT, 1979

Region 1 : Western Europe

	Tourist Receipts $ million	Total GDP $ billion	%
Andorra	3	-	-
Austria	5,603	74	7.6
Belgium*	1,629	116	1.4
Cyprus	141	2	7.1
Denmark	1,312	65	2.0
Finland	534	43	1.2
France	6,826	605	1.1
Germany, West	5,741	809	0.7
Gibraltar	5	-	-
Greece	1,663	37	4.5
Iceland	22	2	1.1
Ireland	527	15	3.5
Italy	8,185	334	2.5
Jersey	179	-	-
Liechtenstein	5	-	-
Luxembourg	*	4	-
Malta	213	1	21.3
Monaco	20	-	-
Netherlands	1,325	157	0.8
Norway	600	48	1.3
Portugal	940	20	4.7
San Marino	2	-	-
Spain	6,484	200	3.2
Sweden	638	110	0.6
Switzerland	2,568	100	2.6
Turkey	281	61	0.5
United Kingdom	5,996	421	1.4
TOTAL	51,442	3,224	1.6

Source: IMF/UN/WTO/OECD/National Offices/Own Estimates.

Table 12. TOURIST EXPENDITURE AS A PROPORTION OF TOTAL PRIVATE CONSUMER EXPENDITURE, 1979

Region 1 : Western Europe

	Tourist Expenditure ($ million)	Total Private Expenditure ($ billion)	%
Andorra	5	-	
Austria	2,966	37.0	8.0
Belgium	2,969	64.8	4.6
Cyprus	45	1.2	3.8
Denmark	1,542	33.8	4.6
Finland	489	23.1	2.1
France	5,191	334.1	1.6
Germany, West	17,952	391.2	4.6
Gibraltar	-	-	-
Greece	202	19.6	1.0
Iceland	39	0.1	39.0
Ireland	518	8.6	6.0
Italy	1,507	181.4	0.8
Jersey	-	-	-
Liechtenstein	3	-	-
Luxembourg	*	2.2	-
Malta	21	0.6	3.5
Monaco	6	-	-
Netherlands	4,804	81.2	5.9
Norway	1,154	22.2	5.2
Portugal	245	11.2	2.2
San Marino	-	-	-
Spain	922	107.9	0.9
Sweden	1,750	55.5	3.2
Switzerland	2,030	57.2	3.5
Turkey	95	4.7	2.0
United Kingdom	4,497	275.6	1.6
TOTAL	**48,952**	**1,713.2**	**2.9**

Source: IMF/UN/WTO/OECD/National Offices/Own Estimates.

Table 13.   **TOURIST RECEIPTS**

Region 2 : Eastern Europe

($ millions)	1976	1977	1978	1979	1980
Albania	1	1	2	2	2
Bulgaria	230	235	240	250	255
Czechoslovakia	156	184	352	385	380
East Germany	100	120	120	150	150
Hungary	263	320	415	452	480
Poland	157	170	224	261	280
Romania	112	118	121	125	136
USSR	225	250	275	300	325
Yugoslavia	802	915	1,131	1,183	1,220
TOTAL	2,046	2,313	2,880	3,108	3,228

Source: IMF/UN/WTO/OECD/National Offices/Own Estimates.

Table 14.   **TOURIST EXPENDITURE**

Region 2 : Eastern Europe

($ million)	1976	1977	1978	1979	1980
Albania	2	3	3	4	4
Bulgaria	31	33	37	38	40
Czechoslovakia	156	184	262	276	290
East Germany	180	200	225	250	270
Hungary	144	167	190	190	196
Poland	213	256	319	352	380
Romania	27	28	30	31	32
USSR	125	140	160	185	200
Yugoslavia	77	98	128	155	170
TOTAL	955	1,109	1,354	1,481	1,582

Source: IMF/UN/WTO/OECD/National Offices/Own Estimates.

Table 15. **BALANCE OF TOURISM PAYMENTS**

Region 2 : Eastern Europe

($ million)	1976	1977	1978	1979	1980
Albania	− 1	− 2	− 1	− 2	− 2
Bulgaria	199	202	203	212	215
Czechoslovakia	0	0	90	109	90
East Germany	− 80	− 80	− 105	− 100	− 120
Hungary	119	153	225	262	284
Poland	− 56	− 86	− 95	− 91	− 100
Romania	85	90	91	94	104
USSR	100	110	115	115	125
Yugoslavia	725	817	1,003	1,028	1,050
TOTAL	1,091	1,204	1,526	1,627	1,646

Source: IMF/UN/WTO/OECD/National Offices/Own Estimates.

Table 16.   TOURIST RECEIPTS AS A PROPORTION OF GROSS DOMESTIC PRODUCT, 1979

Region 2 : Eastern Europe

	Tourist Receipts $ million	Total GDP $ billion	%
Albania	2	2[1]	0.1
Bulgaria	250	20	1.3
Czechoslovakia	385	44	0.9
East Germany	150	126	0.1
Hungary	452	28	1.6
Poland	261	58	0.5
Romania	125	42	0.3
USSR	300	674	0.1
Yugoslavia	1,183	61	1.9
TOTAL	3,108	1,055	0.3

(1)   GNP.

Source: IMF/UN/WTO/OECD/National Offices/Own Estimates.

Table 17.   TOURIST EXPENDITURE AS A PROPORTION OF TOTAL PRIVATE CONSUMER EXPENDITURE, 1979

Region 2 : Eastern Europe

	Tourist Expenditure ($ million)	Total Private Expenditure ($ billion)	%
Albania	4	-	-
Bulgaria	38	14.1	0.3
Czechoslovakia	276	27.3	1.0
East Germany	250	107.0	0.2
Hungary	190	16.9	1.1
Poland	352	45.5	0.8
Romania	31	20.0	0.2
USSR	185	492.4	0.1
Yugoslavia	155	21.2	0.7
TOTAL	1,481	744.4	0.2

Source: IMF/UN/WTO/OECD/National Offices/Own Estimates.

Table 18   TOURIST RECEIPTS

Region 3 : North & Central America

($ million)	1976	1977	1978	1979	1980
Antigua	25	30	36	45	60
Aruba	50	60	75	85	115
Bahamas	368	372	490	552	650
Barbados	83	111	138	207	252
Belize	24	29	30	34	35
Bermuda	192	230	195	240	258
Bonaire	6	7	7	8	8
British Virgin Isles	30	36	44	55	70
Canada	1,972	1,901	2,078	2,470	2,861
Costa Rica	55	62	72	74	87
Cuba	20	32	40	48	60
Grenada	8	10	12	15	16
Guadeloupe	23	24	27	30	32
Guatemala	66	66	67	82	62
Haiti	25	30	54	72	65
Honduras	12	14	17	21	24
Jamaica	106	106	147	195	242
Martinique	40	50	62	88	100
Mexico	2,233	2,121	3,206	4,132	5,220
Montserrat	3	3	4	4	5
Netherlands Antilles	190	207	271	317	340
Nicaragua	28	34	25	18	20
Panama	124	132	146	166	180
Puerto Rico	393	482	547	570	600
St. Kitts	7	10	11	12	13
St. Vincent	9	13	14	16	18
Trinidad & Tobago	87	89	92	124	136
U.S.A.	5,738	6,164	7,199	8,346	10,087
TOTAL	11,917	12,425	15,106	18,026	21,616

Source: IMF/UN/WTO/OECD/National Offices/Own Estimates.

Table 19.   **TOURIST EXPENDITURE**

Region 3 : North & Central America

($ million)	1976	1977	1978	1979	1980
Antigua	16	18	21	24	27
Aruba					
Bahamas	44	55	61	53	71
Barbados	8	9	10	13	19
Belize	4	5	6	7	7
Bermuda	1	1	2	2	2
Bonaire	-	1	1	1	1
British Virgin Isles	-	-	-	1	1
Canada	3,167	3,466	3,607	3,377	3,914
Costa Rica	42	51	62	63	62
Cuba	128	138	150	170	192
Grenada	-	1	4	7	10
Guadeloupe	8	10	10	11	13
Guatemala	82	100	107	120	164
Haiti	5	6	12	13	28
Honduras	16	21	23	29	31
Jamaica	59	12	10	11	12
Martinique	7	9	9	10	11
Mexico	1,617	1,183	2,147	2,934	4,187
Montserrat	2	3	3	4	4
Netherlands Antilles	38	41	43	52	58
Nicaragua	35	46	60	48	52
Panama	34	35	37	39	40
Puerto Rico	238	225	337	350	360
St. Kitts	-	1	1	1	1
St. Vincent	1	1	1	2	2
Trinidad & Tobago	37	52	67	86	95
U.S.A.	6,856	7,451	8,475	9,413	10,399
TOTAL	12,445	12,941	15,266	16,841	19,763

Source: IMF/UN/WTO/OECD/National Offices/Own Estimates.

Table 20.   BALANCE OF TOURISM PAYMENTS

Region 3 : North & Central America

($ million)	1976	1977	1978	1979	1980
Antigua	9	12	15	21	33
Aruba	50	60	75	85	115
Bahamas	324	317	429	499	579
Barbados	75	102	128	194	233
Belize	20	24	24	27	28
Bermuda	191	229	193	238	256
Bonaire	6	6	6	7	7
British Virgin Isles	30	36	44	54	69
Canada	−1,195	−1,565	−1,529	− 907	−1,053
Costa Rica	13	11	10	11	25
Cuba	− 108	− 106	− 110	− 122	− 132
Grenada	8	9	8	8	6
Guadeloupe	15	14	17	19	19
Guatemala	− 16	− 34	− 40	− 38	− 102
Haiti	20	24	42	59	37
Honduras	− 4	− 7	− 6	− 8	− 7
Jamaica	47	94	137	184	230
Martinique	33	41	53	78	89
Mexico	616	938	1,059	1,198	1,033
Montserrat	1	0	1	0	1
Netherlands Antilles	152	166	228	265	282
Nicaragua	− 7	− 12	− 35	− 30	− 32
Panama	90	97	109	127	140
Puerto Rico	155	257	210	220	240
St. Kitts	7	9	10	11	12
St. Vincent	8	12	13	14	16
Trinidad & Tobago	50	37	25	38	41
U.S.A.	−1,118	−1,287	−1,276	−1,067	− 312
TOTAL	− 528	− 516	− 160	1,185	1,853

Source: IMF/UN/WTO/OECD/National Offices/Own Estimates.

Table 21. TOURIST RECEIPTS AS A PROPORTION OF GROSS DOMESTIC PRODUCT, 1979

Region 3 : North & Central America

	Tourist Receipts $ million	Total GDP $ billion	%
Antigua	45	85[1]	0.1
Aruba	85	20	0.4
Bahamas	552	1	55.2
Barbados	207	1	20.7
Belize	34	-	11.3
Bermuda	240	1[1]	24.0
Bonaire	8	1	8.0
British Virgin Isles	55	-	55.0
Canada	2,470	228	1.1
Costa Rica	74	4	1.9
Cuba	48	14[1]	0.3
Grenada	15	60[1]	-
Guadeloupe	30	1[1]	3.0
Guatemala	82	7	1.2
Haiti	72	1	7.2
Honduras	21	2	1.1
Jamaica	195	2	9.8
Martinique	88	1	8.8
Mexico	4,132	121	3.4
Montserrat	4	-	4.0
Netherlands Antilles	317	1	31.7
Nicaragua	18	1	1.8
Panama	166	3	5.5
Puerto Rico	570	14	4.1
St. Kitts	12	-	12.0
St. Vincent	16	-	16.0
Trinidad & Tobago	124	5	24.8
U.S.A.	8,346	2,350	0.4
TOTAL	18,026	2,924	0.6

(1) GNP.

Source: IMF/UN/WTO/OECD/National Offices/Own Estimates.

34

Table 22. TOURIST EXPENDITURE AS A PROPORTION OF TOTAL PRIVATE CONSUMER EXPENDITURE, 1979

Region 3 : North & Central America

	Tourist Expenditure ($ million)	Total Private Expenditure ($ billion)	%
Antigua	24	1.0	2.4
Aruba	-	-	-
Bahamas	53	0.6	8.8
Barbados	13	0.9	1.4
Belize	7	0.1	7.0
Bermuda	2	2.0	0.1
Bonaire	1	0.1	1.0
British Virgin Isles	1	0.1	1.0
Canada	3,377	127.4	2.7
Costa Rica	63	2.7	2.3
Cuba	170	8.7	2.0
Grenada	7	0.1	7.0
Guadeloupe	11	0.8	1.4
Guatemala	120	5.4	2.2
Haiti	13	1.0	13.0
Honduras	29	1.4	2.1
Jamaica	11	2.3	0.5
Martinique	10	1.0	1.0
Mexico	2,934	75.6	3.9
Montserrat	4	0.1	4.0
Netherlands Antilles	52	0.5	10.4
Nicaragua	48	1.6	3.0
Panama	39	1.9	2.1
Puerto Rico	350	11.1	3.2
St. Kitts	1	0.1	1.0
St. Vincent	2	0.1	2.0
Trinidad & Tobago	86	1.7	5.1
U.S.A.	9,413	1,509.8	0.6
TOTAL	16,841	1,758.1	1.0

Source: IMF/UN/WTO/OECD/National Offices/Own Estimates.

Table 23.   **TOURIST RECEIPTS**

Region 4 : South America

($ million)	1976	1977	1978	1979	1980
Argentina	180	212	280	267	344
Bolivia	26	29	35	37	40
Brazil	57	55	68	75	126
Colombia	188	245	283	358	357
Chile	87	82	109	150	174
Dominican Republic	71	84	88	116	132
Ecuador	31	48	65	80	91
El Salvador	21	32	37	42	45
Guyana	3	3	3	3	4
Paraguay	14	35	40	69	91
Peru	99	111	141	189	210
Suriname	11	13	18	21	19
Uruguay	60	96	109	136	150
Venezuela	109	168	205	178	246
TOTAL	957	1,213	1,481	1,721	2,029

Source: IMF/UN/WTO/OECD/National Offices/Own Estimates.

Table 24.　　　　　　　　**TOURIST EXPENDITURE**

Region 4 : South America

($ million)	1976	1977	1978	1979	1980
Argentina	114	175	309	362	425
Bolivia	31	38	41	45	52
Brazil	470	357	388	466	500
Colombia	174	200	229	236	250
Chile	88	205	130	165	195
Dominican Republic	84	88	101	112	121
Ecuador	50	82	97	129	149
El Salvador	43	58	103	117	130
Guyana	6	3	5	6	8
Paraguay	13	16	20	31	35
Peru	57	36	34	45	48
Suriname	16	19	23	32	33
Uruguay	60	96	109	136	158
Venezuela	617	980	1,545	1,658	1,879
TOTAL	1,823	2,353	3,134	3,540	3,983

Source: IMF/UN/WTO/OECD/National Offices/Own Estimates.

Table 25.   **BALANCE OF TOURISM PAYMENTS**

Region 4 : South America

($ million)	1976	1977	1978	1979	1980
Argentina	66	37	− 29	− 95	− 81
Bolivia	− 5	− 9	− 6	− 8	− 12
Brazil	−413	− 302	− 320	− 391	− 374
Colombia	14	45	− 120	− 86	− 76
Chile	− 1	− 123	− 21	− 15	− 21
Dominican Republic	− 13	− 4	− 13	4	11
Ecuador	− 19	− 34	33	− 49	− 58
Guyana	− 22	− 26	− 66	− 75	− 85
Paraguay	1	19	20	38	56
Peru	42	75	107	144	162
Suriname	− 5	− 6	− 5	− 11	− 14
Uruguay	0	0	0	0	− 8
Venezuela	−508	− 812	−1,340	−1,480	−1,633
TOTAL	−866	−1,140	−1,653	−1,819	−1,954

Source: IMF/UN/WTO/OECD/National Offices/Own Estimates.

Table 26. TOURIST RECEIPTS AS A PROPORTION OF GROSS
DOMESTIC PRODUCT, 1979

Region 4 : South America

	Tourist Receipts $ million	Total GDP $ billion	%
Argentina	267	95	0.3
Bolivia	37	4	0.9
Brazil	75	134	0.1
Colombia	358	27	1.3
Chile	150	20	0.8
Dominican Republic	116	5	2.3
Ecuador	80	9	0.9
El Salvador	42	4	1.1
Guyana	3	2	0.2
Paraguay	69	3	2.3
Peru	189	13	1.5
Suriname	21	1	2.1
Uruguay	136	7	1.9
Venezuela	178	49	0.4
TOTAL	1,721	373	0.6

Source: IMF/UN/WTO/OECD/National Offices/Own Estimates.

Table 27. TOURIST EXPENDITURE AS A PROPORTION OF TOTAL PRIVATE CONSUMER EXPENDITURE, 1979

Region 4 : South America

	Tourist Expenditure ($ million)	Total Private Expenditure ($ billion)	%
Argentina	362	113.6	0.3
Bolivia	45	2.9	1.6
Brazil	466	95.5	0.5
Colombia	236	18.4	1.3
Chile	165	13.5	1.2
Dominican Republic	112	4.1	2.7
Ecuador	129	5.7	2.3
El Salvador	117	2.4	4.9
Guyana	6	0.4	1.5
Paraguay	31	2.5	1.2
Peru	45	8.7	0.5
Suriname	32	0.6	5.3
Uruguay	136	5.1	2.7
Venezuela	1,658	25.4	6.5
TOTAL	3,540	298.8	1.2

Source: IMF/UN/WTO/OECD/National Offices/Own Estimates.

Table 28.		TOURIST RECEIPTS			
Region 5 : North Africa & Middle East					
($ million)	**1976**	**1977**	**1978**	**1979**	**1980**
Algeria	88	100	93	103	64
Bahrain	136	158	178	200	235
Iran	142	152	153	64	25
Iraq	86	89	108	165	180
Israel	431	563	595	798	865
Jordan	207	288	340	444	519
Kuwait	103	144	160	351	377
Lebanon	70	90	110	135	160
Libya	39	8	9	9	9
Morocco	274	333	396	429	453
Oman	25	32	43	57	70
Qatar	112	136	157	180	200
Saudi Arabia	688	825	1,035	1,196	1,343
Syria	100	110	125	136	156
Tunisia	313	335	428	602	682
United Arab Emirates	21	24	36	45	53
Yemen	8	12	12	27	40
Yemen, South	3	3	5	3	4
TOTAL	2,846	3,402	3,983	4,944	5,435

Source: IMF/UN/WTO/OECD/National Offices/Own Estimates.

Table 29.   **TOURIST EXPENDITURE**

Region 5 : North Africa & Middle East

($ million)	1976	1977	1978	1979	1980
Algeria	104	153	198	242	333
Bahrain	180	210	240	270	300
Iran	1,092	1,465	1,211	1,000	1,000
Iraq	250	287	312	336	350
Israel	185	244	346	433	514
Jordan	121	128	208	298	361
Kuwait	249	307	386	826	1,339
Lebanon	95	110	125	140	160
Libya	166	271	260	397	450
Morocco	80	93	105	102	98
Oman	60	80	105	130	160
Qatar	125	160	200	240	270
Saudi Arabia	672	930	2,413	3,037	3,526
Syria	148	70	54	107	177
Tunisia	58	63	88	90	105
United Arab Emirates	26	32	40	48	65
Yemen	7	10	10	22	32
Yemen, South	2	4	4	5	6
TOTAL	3,620	4,617	6,305	7,723	9,246

Source: IMF/UN/WTO/OECD/National Offices/Own Estimates.

Table 30.   **BALANCE OF TOURISM PAYMENTS**

Region 5 : North Africa & Middle East

($ million)	1976	1977	1978	1979	1980
Algeria	− 16	− 53	− 105	− 139	− 269
Bahrain	− 44	− 52	− 62	− 70	− 65
Iran	−950	−1,313	−1,058	− 936	− 975
Iraq	−164	− 198	− 204	− 171	− 170
Israel	246	319	249	365	351
Jordan	86	160	132	146	158
Kuwait	−146	− 163	− 226	− 475	− 962
Lebanon	− 25	− 20	− 15	− 5	0
Libya	−127	− 263	− 251	− 388	− 441
Morocco	194	240	291	327	355
Oman	− 35	− 48	− 62	− 73	− 90
Qatar	− 13	− 24	− 43	− 60	− 70
Saudi Arabia	16	− 105	−1,378	−1,841	−2,183
Syria	− 48	40	71	29	− 21
Tunisia	255	272	340	512	577
United Arab Emirates	− 5	− 8	− 4	− 3	− 12
Yemen	1	2	2	5	8
Yemen, South	1	− 1	− 1	− 2	− 2
TOTAL	−774	−1,215	−2,322	−2,779	−3,811

Source: IMF/UN/WTO/OECD/National Offices/Own Estimates.

Table 31. TOURIST RECEIPTS AS A PROPORTION OF GROSS DOMESTIC PRODUCT, 1979

Region 5 : North Africa & Middle East

	Tourist Receipts $ million	Total GDP $ million	%
Algeria	103	30	0.3
Bahrain	200	2[1]	10.0
Iran	64	92	0.1
Iraq	165	31	0.5
Israel	798	14	5.7
Jordan	444	2	22.2
Kuwait	351	23	1.5
Lebanon	135	3	4.5
Libya	9	25	0.1
Morocco	429	15	2.9
Oman	57	3	1.9
Qatar	180	4[1]	4.5
Saudi Arabia	1,196	74	1.6
Syria	136	10	1.4
Tunisia	602	7	8.6
United Arab Emirates	45	21	0.2
Yemen	27	3	0.9
Yemen, South	3	1	0.3
TOTAL	4,944	360	1.5

(1) GNP.

Source: IMF/UN/WTO/OECD/National Offices/Own Estimates.

Table 32.   TOURIST EXPENDITURE AS A PROPORTION OF TOTAL PRIVATE CONSUMER EXPENDITURE, 1979

Region 5 : North Africa & Middle East

	Tourist Expenditure ($ million)	Total Private Expenditure ($ billion)	%
Algeria	242	12.9	1.9
Bahrain	270	0.8	33.8
Iran	1,000	43.8	2.3
Iraq	336	24.2	1.4
Israel	433	11.0	3.9
Jordan	298	2.1	14.2
Kuwait	826	3.3	25.0
Lebanon	140	3.8	3.7
Libya	397	6.7	5.9
Morocco	102	9.6	1.1
Oman	130	0.9	14.4
Qatar	240	n/a	n/a
Saudi Arabia	3,037	22.5	13.5
Syria	107	7.0	1.5
Tunisia	90	4.5	2.0
United Arab Emirates	48	3.2	1.5
Yemen	22	2.9	0.8
Yemen, South	5	0.5	1.0
TOTAL	7,723	159.8	4.8

Source: IMF/UN/WTO/OECD/National Offices/Own Estimates.

Table 33.   **TOURIST RECEIPTS**

Region 6 : Africa

($ million)	1976	1977	1978	1979	1980
Angola	1	2	2	3	3
Benin	3	3	5	6	8
Botswana	9	10	10	16	24
Burundi	1	1	1	2	2
Cameroon	3	5	10	10	12
Central African Republic	4	4	4	3	4
Chad	9	9	8	7	8
Comoros	1	1	1	1	1
Congo	3	4	5	5	7
Egypt	223	644	586	601	773
Ethiopia	6	6	4	6	7
Gambia	7	8	9	17	18
Ghana	14	11	12	12	13
Ivory Coast	26	32	39	48	60
Kenya	98	120	167	177	224
Lesotho	4	5	5	6	6
Liberia	5	6	6	6	6
Madagascar	3	2	3	5	6
Malawi	5	5	5	5	5
Mali	8	8	8	8	9
Mauritius	28	31	35	41	46
Mozambique	16	18	20	22	25
Namibia	6	7	7	8	8
Niger	2	3	3	3	3
Nigeria	33	97	80	25	55
Senegal	46	52	64	67	70
Seychelles	18	22	32	39	44
South Africa	289	320	367	492	625
Sudan	5	5	5	5	6
Swaziland	28	35	25	32	35
Tanzania	13	9	13	15	17
Togo	4	7	10	11	13
Uganda	2	2	4	9	5
Upper Volta	2	2	6	11	10
Zaire	11	10	20	19	20
Zambia	13	13	13	16	16
TOTAL	949	1,519	1,594	1,759	2,194

Source: IMF/UN/WTO/OECD/National Offices/Own Estimates.

Table 34. TOURIST EXPENDITURE

Region 6 : Africa

($ million)	1976	1977	1978	1979	1980
Angola	8	9	9	10	10
Benin	5	5	6	6	7
Botswana	7	8	9	13	18
Burundi	3	4	4	5	5
Cameroon	39	43	65	69	72
Central African Republic	17	16	19	18	18
Chad	14	19	21	23	26
Comoros	1	2	2	2	3
Congo	26	25	25	29	29
Egypt	124	172	258	248	243
Ethiopia	6	5	3	3	5
Gambia	2	1	1	1	1
Ghana	15	24	25	27	27
Ivory Coast	120	141	177	227	260
Kenya	30	18	40	41	33
Lesotho	2	2	3	3	3
Liberia	4	4	5	5	6
Madagascar	18	18	23	28	33
Malawi	6	7	7	8	10
Mali	18	20	26	18	16
Mauritius	15	17	19	25	22
Mozambique	55	55	76	82	90
Namibia	3	4	4	5	6
Niger	9	10	12	14	16
Nigeria	402	399	300	271	360
Senegal	25	28	34	41	46
Seychelles	2	2	4	6	8
South Africa	388	405	464	578	755
Sudan	31	29	42	42	48
Swaziland	17	18	19	27	25
Tanzania	10	13	14	11	20
Togo	12	14	17	18	20
Uganda	10	14	11	20	18
Upper Volta	12	16	24	25	27
Zaire	23	29	32	36	40
Zambia	17	28	39	37	57
TOTAL	1,496	1,624	1,839	2,022	2,383

Source: IMF/UN/WTO/OECD/National Offices/Own Estimates.

Table 35.   **BALANCE OF TOURISM PAYMENTS**

Region 6 : Africa

($ million)	1976	1977	1978	1979	1980
Angola	− 7	− 7	− 7	− 7	− 7
Benin	− 2	− 2	− 1	0	1
Botswana	2	2	1	3	− 6
Burundi	− 2	− 3	− 3	− 3	− 3
Cameroon	− 36	− 38	− 55	− 59	− 60
Central African Republic	− 13	− 12	− 15	− 15	− 14
Chad	− 5	− 10	− 13	− 16	− 18
Comoros	0	− 1	− 1	− 1	− 2
Congo	− 23	− 21	− 20	− 24	− 22
Egypt	99	472	328	353	530
Ethiopia	0	1	1	3	2
Gambia	5	7	8	16	17
Ghana	− 1	− 13	− 13	− 15	− 14
Ivory Coast	− 94	−109	−138	−179	−200
Kenya	68	102	127	136	191
Lesotho	2	3	2	3	3
Liberia	1	2	1	1	0
Madagascar	− 15	− 16	− 20	− 23	− 27
Malawi	− 1	− 2	− 2	− 3	− 5
Mali	− 10	− 12	− 18	− 10	− 7
Mauritius	13	14	16	16	24
Mozambique	− 39	− 37	− 56	− 60	− 65
Namibia	3	3	3	3	2
Niger	− 7	− 7	− 9	− 11	− 13
Nigeria	−369	−302	−220	−246	−305
Senegal	21	24	30	26	24
Seychelles	16	20	28	33	36
South Africa	− 99	− 85	− 97	− 86	−130
Sudan	− 26	− 24	− 37	− 37	− 42
Swaziland	11	18	6	5	10
Tanzania	3	− 4	− 1	4	− 3
Togo	− 8	− 7	− 7	− 7	− 7
Uganda	− 8	− 12	− 7	− 11	− 13
Upper Volta	− 10	− 14	− 18	− 14	− 17
Zaire	− 12	− 19	− 12	− 26	− 20
Zambia	− 4	− 15	− 26	− 21	− 41
TOTAL	547	105	245	263	189

Source: IMF/UN/WTO/OECD/National Offices/Own Estimates.

Table 36. **TOURIST RECEIPTS AS A PROPORTION OF GROSS DOMESTIC PRODUCT, 1979**

Region 6 : Africa

	Tourist Receipts $ million	Total GDP $ billion	%
Angola	3	3	0.1
Benin	6	1	0.6
Botswana	16	1	1.6
Burundi	2	1	0.2
Cameroon	10	5	0.2
Central African Republic	3	1	0.3
Chad	7	1	0.7
Comoros	1	-	0.5
Congo	5	1	0.5
Egypt	601	18	3.3
Ethiopia	6	4	0.2
Gambia	17	-	8.5
Ghana	12	10	0.1
Ivory Coast	48	9	0.5
Kenya	177	6	3.0
Lesotho	6	-	2.0
Liberia	6	1	0.6
Madagascar	5	3	0.2
Malawi	5	1	0.5
Mali	8	1	0.8
Mauritius	41	1	4.1
Mozambique	22	2	1.1
Namibia	8	-	2.0
Niger	3	2	0.2
Nigeria	25	75	0.1
Senegal	67	3	2.2
Seychelles	39	-	39.0
South Africa	492	58	0.8
Sudan	5	8	0.1
Swaziland	32	-	8.0
Tanzania	15	5	0.3
Togo	11	1	1.1
Uganda	9	8	0.1
Upper Volta	11	1	1.1
Zaire	19	6	0.3
Zambia	16	3	0.5
TOTAL	1,759	240	0.7

Source: IMF/UN/WTO/OECD/National Offices/Own Estimates.

Table 37. TOURIST EXPENDITURE AS A PROPORTION OF TOTAL PRIVATE CONSUMER EXPENDITURE, 1979

Region 6 : Africa

	Tourist Expenditure ($ million)	Total Private Expenditure ($ billion)	%
Angola	10	1.1	0.9
Benin	6	1.2	0.5
Botswana	13	0.5	2.6
Burundi	5	0.6	0.8
Cameroon	69	4.3	1.6
Central African Republic	18	0.3	6.0
Chad	23	0.8	2.9
Comoros	2	0.1	2.0
Congo	29	0.8	3.6
Egypt	248	12.3	2.0
Ethiopia	3	2.5	0.1
Gambia	1	0.1	1.0
Ghana	27	7.0	0.4
Ivory Coast	227	5.1	4.5
Kenya	41	4.0	1.0
Lesotho	3	0.2	1.5
Liberia	5	0.4	1.3
Madagascar	28	1.7	1.6
Malawi	8	0.7	1.1
Mali	18	0.2	9.0
Mauritius	25	0.5	5.0
Mozambique	82	2.0	4.1
Namibia	5	0.2	2.5
Niger	14	1.1	1.3
Nigeria	271	37.5	0.7
Senegal	41	2.0	2.1
Seychelles	6	0.1	6.0
South Africa	578	30.3	1.9
Sudan	42	9.0	0.5
Swaziland	27	0.3	9.0
Tanzania	11	3.5	0.3
Togo	18	0.7	2.6
Uganda	20	1.3	1.5
Upper Volta	25	0.8	3.1
Zaire	36	4.1	0.9
Zambia	37	1.6	0.9
TOTAL	2,022	138.9	1.5

Source: IMF/UN/WTO/OECD/National Offices/Own Estimates

Table 38. **TOURIST RECEIPTS**

Region 7 : Far East

($ million)	1976	1977	1978	1979	1980
Afghanistan	30	38	28	7	8
Bangladesh	4	5	6	10	16
Bhutan		1	1	2	2
Brunei	1	2	2	3	3
Burma	3	3	5	7	8
China	12	30	60	80	100
Guam	120	145	170	200	235
Hong Kong	740	786	1,110	1,276	1,350
India	250	350	403	422	455
Indonesia	62	88	131	209	246
Japan	312	420	463	556	638
Korea, South	275	370	408	327	370
Laos	3	4	5	6	6
Macau	27	30	34	37	41
Malaysia	137	165	199	240	273
Maldives	16	21	22	25	30
Mongolia	38	47	58	60	72
Nepal	21	26	34	45	63
Pakistan	39	55	78	97	148
Philippines	92	145	210	238	320
Samoa	4	4	4	4	4
Singapore	513	622	777	1,121	1,320
Sri Lanka	23	33	48	68	99
Taiwan	466	527	608	919	1,150
Thailand	197	205	435	549	709
TOTAL	3,385	4,122	5,299	6,508	7,666

Source: IMF/UN/WTO/OECD/National Offices/Own Estimates.

Table 39.   **TOURIST EXPENDITURE**

Region 7 : Far East

($ million)	1976	1977	1978	1979	1980
Afghanistan	2	3	3	4	5
Bangladesh	5	3	13	16	16
Bhutan	-	-	1	1	1
Brunei	-	1	1	1	2
Burma	1	2	2	3	3
China	280	335	370	425	500
Guam	1	2	2	3	3
Hong Kong	300	370	460	560	700
India	38	51	80	120	136
Indonesia	135	131	274	366	375
Japan	1,662	2,148	3,693	4,806	4,594
Korea, South	46	102	207	404	350
Laos	5	5	6	6	7
Macau	2	3	3	3	4
Malaysia	196	244	336	398	470
Maldives	-	1	1	2	2
Mongolia	5	6	6	7	7
Nepal	13	15	18	22	26
Pakistan	62	55	66	96	85
Philippines	29	35	51	75	105
Samoa	-	2	2	3	3
Singapore	220	270	335	400	470
Sri Lanka	12	13	15	18	23
Taiwan	180	230	300	350	425
Thailand	120	145	180	235	275
TOTAL	3,314	4,172	6,425	8,324	8,587

Source: IMF/UN/WTO/OECD/National Offices/Own Estimates.

Table 40. BALANCE OF TOURISM PAYMENTS

Region 7 : Far East

($ million)	1976	1977	1978	1979	1980
Afghanistan	28	35	25	3	3
Bangladesh	− 1	− 2	− 7	− 6	0
Bhutan	-	1	0	1	1
Brunei	1	1	1	2	1
Burma	2	1	3	4	5
China	− 268	− 305	− 310	− 345	− 400
Guam	119	143	168	197	232
Hong Kong	440	416	650	716	650
India	212	299	323	302	319
Indonesia	− 73	− 43	− 143	− 157	− 129
Japan	−1,352	−1,728	−3,230	−4,250	−3,956
Korea, South	229	268	201	− 77	20
Laos	− 2	− 1	− 1	0	− 1
Macau	25	27	31	34	37
Malaysia	− 59	− 79	− 137	− 158	− 197
Maldives	16	20	21	23	28
Mongolia	33	41	52	33	65
Nepal	8	11	16	23	37
Pakistan	− 23	0	12	1	63
Philippines	63	110	159	163	215
Samoa	4	2	2	1	1
Singapore	293	352	442	721	850
Sri Lanka	11	20	33	50	76
Taiwan	286	297	308	569	725
Thailand	77	60	255	314	434
TOTAL	71	− 50	−1,126	−1,816	−1,021

Source: IMF/UN/WTO/OECD/National Offices/Own Estimates.

Table 41.   TOURIST RECEIPTS AS A PROPORTION OF GROSS DOMESTIC PRODUCT, 1979

Region 7 : Far East

	Tourist Receipts $ million	Total GDP $ billion	%
Afghanistan	7	4	0.2
Bangladesh	10	10	0.1
Bhutan	2	1(1)	0.2
Brunei	3	3	0.1
Burma	7	5	0.1
China	80	252	-
Guam	200	1(1)	20.0
Hong Kong	1,276	17	7.5
India	422	112	0.4
Indonesia	209	49	0.4
Japan	556	914	0.1
Korea, South	327	61	0.5
Laos	6	1(1)	0.6
Macau	37	1(1)	3.7
Malaysia	240	20	1.2
Maldives	25	-	-
Mongolia	60	2(1)	3.0
Nepal	45	2	2.3
Pakistan	97	23	0.4
Philippines	238	30	0.8
Samoa	4	-	-
Singapore	1,121	9	12.5
Sri Lanka	68	3	2.3
Taiwan	919	32	2.9
Thailand	549	27	2.0
TOTAL	6,508	1,579	0.4

(1)   GNP

Source: IMF/UN/WTO/OECD/National Offices/Own Estimates.

Table 42.   TOURIST EXPENDITURE AS A PROPORTION OF TOTAL PRIVATE CONSUMER EXPENDITURE, 1979

Region 7 : Far East

	Tourist Expenditure ($ million)	Total Private Expenditure ($ billion)	%
Afghanistan	4	2.6	0.2
Bangladesh	16	8.4	0.2
Bhutan	1	0.1	1.0
Brunei	1	3.0	0.1
Burma	3	4.5	0.1
China	425	164.0	0.3
Guam	3	0.2	1.5
Hong Kong	560	11.8	4.7
India	120	92.5	0.1
Indonesia	366	28.8	1.3
Japan	4,806	531.2	0.9
Korea, South	404	37.4	1.1
Laos	6	1.1	0.5
Macau	3	0.4	0.8
Malaysia	398	10.3	3.9
Maldives	2	-	-
Mongolia	7	-	-
Nepal	22	1.5	1.5
Pakistan	96	19.3	0.5
Philippines	75	19.2	0.4
Samoa	3	0.1	3.0
Singapore	400	5.4	7.4
Sri Lanka	18	2.6	0.7
Taiwan	350	16.2	2.2
Thailand	235	17.3	1.4
TOTAL	8,324	977.9	0.9

Source: IMF/UN/WTO/OECD/National Offices/Own Estimates.

Table 43.   **TOURIST EXPENDITURE**

Region 8 : Oceania

($ million)	1976	1977	1978	1979	1980
Australia	1,163	1,158	1,367	1,544	1,758
Cayman Islands	-	-	-	-	-
Cook Islands	1	1	2	2	2
Fiji	12	13	15	16	17
French Polynesia	2	2	3	3	4
Hawaii	1	2	2	2	2
New Caledonia	1	1	1	2	2
New Zealand	233	286	378	500	541
Papua New Guinea	20	21	19	17	18
Solomon Islands	-	-	-	1	1
Tonga	1	1	1	1	1
Vanuatu	1	1	2	2	2
Western Samoa	-	-	1	1	1
TOTAL	1,435	1,486	1,791	2,091	2,349

Source: IMF/UN/WTO/OECD/National Offices/Own Estimates.

Table 44.   **TOURIST RECEIPTS**

Region 8 : Oceania

($ million)	1976	1977	1978	1979	1980
Australia	350	391	518	747	1,041
Cayman Islands	25	30	20	30	35
Cook Islands	3	4	4	4	4
Fiji	85	87	102	124	135
French Polynesia	49	54	60	66	70
Hawaii	1,450	1,522	2,188	2,620	3,270
New Caledonia	20	24	30	32	36
New Zealand	156	158	168	190	213
Papua New Guinea	8	7	6	9	12
Solomon Islands	1	2	2	2	3
Tonga	2	4	4	5	5
Vanuatu	20	24	30	35	40
Western Samoa	7	6	8	10	13
TOTAL	2,176	2,313	3,140	3,874	4,877

Source: IMF/UN/WTO/OECD/National Offices/Own Estimates.

Table 45.   **BALANCE OF TOURISM PAYMENTS**

Region 8 : Oceania

($ millions)	1976	1977	1978	1979	1980
Australia	− 813	− 767	− 849	− 797	− 717
Cayman Islands	25	30	20	30	35
Cook Islands	2	3	2	2	2
Fiji	73	74	87	108	118
French Polynesia	47	52	57	63	66
Hawaii	1,449	1,520	2,186	2,618	3,268
New Caledonia	19	23	29	30	34
New Zealand	− 77	− 128	− 210	− 310	− 328
Papua New Guinea	− 12	− 14	− 13	− 8	− 6
Solomon Islands	1	2	2	1	2
Tonga	1	3	3	4	4
Vanuatu	19	23	28	33	38
Western Samoa	7	6	7	9	12
TOTAL	741	827	1,349	1,783	2,528

Source: IMF/UN/WTO/OECD/National Offices/Own Estimates.

Table 46.   **TOURIST RECEIPTS AS A PROPORTION OF GROSS DOMESTIC PRODUCT, 1979**

Region 8 : Oceania

	Tourist Receipts $ million	Total GDP $ billion	%
Australia	747	124	0.6
Cayman Islands	30	-	-
Cook Islands	4	-	-
Fiji	124	1	12.4
French Polynesia	66	-	22.0
Hawaii	2,620	-	-
New Caledonia	32	-	8.0
New Zealand	190	20	1.0
Papua New Guinea	9	2	0.5
Solomon Islands	2	-	2.0
Tonga	5	-	5.0
Vanuatu	35	-	35.0
Western Samoa	10	-	10.0
TOTAL	3,874	147	2.6

(1)   GNP

Source: IMF/UN/WTO/OECD/National Offices/Own Estimates.

**Table 47.   TOURIST EXPENDITURE AS A PROPORTION OF TOTAL
PRIVATE CONSUMER EXPENDITURE, 1979**

Region 8 : Oceania

	Tourist Expenditure ($ million)	Total Private Expenditure ($ billion)	%
Australia	1,544	76.4	2.0
Cayman Islands	-	-	-
Cook Islands	2	-	-
Fiji	16	0.6	2.7
French Polynesia	3	0.8	0.4
Hawaii	2	-	-
New Caledonia	2	0.6	0.3
New Zealand	500	12.2	4.1
Papua New Guinea	17	1.2	1.4
Solomon Islands	1	0.1	1.0
Tonga	1	-	-
Vanuatu	2	-	-
Western Samoa	1	-	-
TOTAL	2,091	91.9	2.3

Source: IMF/UN/WTO/OECD/National Offices/Own Estimates.

INTERNATIONAL FINANCIAL SERVICES

As the world travel market has expanded, so has the need for financial services to ease the burden of payment and increase the security of carrying money. This need has seen the growth of two related financial markets which operate on a world scale — the markets for travellers cheques and credit cards.

In 1981, worldwide sales of **travellers cheques** amounted to around $40 billion, of which a large proportion — probably 65% — was accounted for by U.S. sales. Much of this was for internal use, as the U.S. does not possess a branch banking system, and a truer estimate of international sales would probably be in the region of $25 billion.

Table 48.   World Market for Travellers Cheques 1981

	$ Billion	%
North America	25	62.5%
Europe	8	20.0%
Other	7	17.5%
Total	40	100.0%

Source: Own Estimates

The market has grown steadily, but not spectacularly, at a rate of 10-15% per annum over recent years, under the domination of the U.S. company, American Express. They have about 50% of the world market, although again, their domestic U.S. sales must account for a large proportion of the total. Other major companies include Citibank and Bank of America in the U.S.A., and Barclays and Thomas Cook in the United Kingdom, with shares of 5-12% each.

In 1981, the two main credit card companies entered the travellers cheque market, and seem set to stir things up considerably. The first is Visa, who began to market cheques through Chase Manhattan in the States, and Barclays and Trustee Savings in the U.K., and Mastercard who entered into a joint venture with a number of European banks to form Euro Travellers Cheques Inc.

These two arrangement incorporate the two main U.K. issuers of travellers cheques, Barclays (with Visa) and Thomas Cook (in the Euro Travellers Cheque scheme), and these would appear to present considerable competition to American Express. The latter, conscious of their States-orientated bias, have concluded arrangements with three

Table 49. Estimated World Market Shares: Travellers' Cheques 1981

American Express	45%
Visa / Barclays	10%
ETC / Mastercard	8%
Bank of America	8%
Citibank	7%
Others	22%
Total	100%

Source: Own Estimates

leading French banks, Lloyds in the U.K., and a number of German savings banks to consolidate their strength in Europe. This boost in competition will undoubtedly lead to greater promotional efforts, and a considerable expansion in cheque sales would seem on the cards. Developments in the travellers cheque market go hand in hand with those in the **credit card** market, involving as they do, the same protaginists. In 1981, an estimated $100 billion was spent on buying goods via credit cards, about 40% in North America. There are currently about 225 million credit cards in operation.

Table 50. Goods Purchased by Credit Cards 1981

	$ Billion
North America	40
Europe	15
Other	10
Total	65

Source: Own Estimates

The leading credit card firm is Visa, with about 90 million cardholders worldwide, over 3 million outlets taking their cards, and 100,000 offices. Visa have about 45% of the world credit card market.

Mastercard are best known in the U.S.A., and known as Access in the U.K. They have about 70 million members worldwide, and an estimated 33% market share.

American Express, who have a strong domination of travellers cheque sales, have about 5% of the credit card market. Along with Diners Club and Carte Blanche, they are upmarket cards with a high credit limit, and are promoted more for convenience than as a credit instrument.

Table 51. Estimated World Market Shares: Credit Cards 1981

Visa	40%
Mastercard / Access	30%
American Express	5%
Diners Club	2%
Others	23%
Total	100%

Source: Own Estimates

The Europeans have begun to contest the credit card market with their "Eurocard" system but this has had little worldwide impact. The market continues to be dominated by the U.S. firms, with European banks and financial houses happy to arrange deals with them rather than start up a system of their own.

The worldwide use of such paying instruments as travellers cheques and credit cards is constantly increasing, and as the world moves towards a cashless society, they will continue to do so. And if such financial services seek to extend their scope beyond the confines of world travel, they must certainly appreciate the international traveller as their biggest and most valued customer.

CHAPTER FOUR
MAJOR REGIONAL TRENDS

In Chapter Three, we looked at the value of the world travel market, and considered how it had grown over the last five years. Now, using the eight regional breakdowns defined in the introductory notes, I want to look in more detail at the main regional trends, and the total number of world tourist trips. We shall be examining the number of tourist arrivals and the time spent by tourists in every country in the world which actively encourages tourism.

Considerable problems exist in attempting to present comparative international statistics on tourism, and there are discrepancies between my evaluation of total world travel, and that supplied by the World Tourism Organisation. The difficulties relate to the differing ways by which statistics on tourist visitors are collected by countries; some are based on tourist arrivals at frontiers, some on sample surveys or one-off research studies, and some on the number of tourists staying at registered accommodation. Neither the World Tourism Organisation nor the O.E.C.D. appear to attempt to reconcile these differences; certainly they do not do so in their publications. And if we go to the individual national sources — the statistical offices and tourist boards — we can see why. Basically, completely compatible figures are not available, and the only course of action is to present the figures as being incompatible with an excessive list of notes pointing out all the discrepancies in collection.

Rather than adopt this approach, I have heavily used estimates in order to attempt to provide reasonably comparable statistics on tourist arrivals, nights and length of stay, and this is why my figures are different to those which have gone before. It seemed more logical, for the purposes of this book, to present partly-estimated tabulations which in my opinion provide a much truer overall picture of the structure of world demand.

The first calculation was to exclude anyone who was not technically a "tourist", using the W.T.O. definition. Many countries give figures on the number of visitors arriving in the country, but this includes various categories which are not tourists — transit visitors, cruise visitors, same-day excursionists, and persons coming to the country for a lengthy stay, such as some students and businessmen.

The second was to try to differentiate between tourist arrivals at frontiers, and tourist arrivals at registered accommodation. Though a tourist may arrive in a country, they may not stay in registered accommodation; most obviously, they may stay with friends or relatives.

Europe was best documented in this regard, although there was still considerable gaps in the figures available. For this region alone, I have tabulated three different sets of statistics — firstly, arrivals at frontiers, arrivals at all registered accommodation (including supplementary) and arrivals at hotels and so forth. I have also compiled a table on the number of nights spent in all registered accommodation, and again, just for hotels. The average length of stay is based on the number of arrivals in registered accommodation divided into the number of nights in the same.

Unfortunately, these breakdowns were not widely available outside Europe, and to attempt to provide a similar analysis would have involved an excessive amount of estimation. For the remaining regions, therefore, the figures cover the number of tourist visits, and the number of tourist nights, the average length of stay being calculated from these.

I think on the whole that the tourist visits for the regions outside Europe are reasonably compatible with the tourist arrivals at frontiers within Europe. The difference between frontier arrivals and arrivals at registered accommodation is likely to be less outside Europe, with the exception of the major countries such as the U.S.A., Canada, Australia etc. In other words, most tourists visiting, say, the Far East, would stay in registered accommodation. But there is a difference here and this should be made clear; it may not affect the overall arrival figures, but it does effect the number of nights and the length of stay.

THE WORLD MARKET

In 1980, a total of 350 million tourists trips were taken around the world, staying for a total of 1.7 billion nights — an average of about five nights per visit. Assuming that a proportion of these were repeat trips by the same people, we can roughly estimate that 7% of the world's population entered other countries as tourists in 1980.

In 1981, tourist trips are estimated to have increased further to 365 million, a 3% increase over 1980.

Table 52.   World Market for Tourism 1976-1981

(million)	World Population	Tourist Visits	%
1975	4,050	282	7.0
1976	4,107	294	7.2
1977	4,182	312	7.5
1978	4,258	324	7.6
1979	4,336	346	8.0
1980	4,415	355	8.0
1981e	4,500	365	8.1

Source: Own Calculations

66

Table 53.   Total Population of Countries Covered

(millions)	1975	1976	1977	1978	1979	1980
Western Europe	384.70	386.75	388.87	391.10	393.55	395.54
Eastern Europe	384.44	387.69	390.97	394.08	397.20	400.09
North and Central America	333.57	338.49	343.62	348.35	353.76	364.88
South America	216.17	221.75	227.52	233.35	239.36	246.59
North Africa and Middle East	119.96	122.97	126.92	129.82	134.26	137.78
Africa	338.80	349.17	359.74	370.27	381.13	391.82
Far East	2,120.98	2,160.08	2,199.05	2,237.24	2,276.74	2,316.50
Oceania	21.88	22.15	22.44	22.72	23.01	23.25
Total	3,920.50	3,989.05	4,059.13	4,126.93	4,199.01	4,276.45
Total World Population	4,050.00	4,107.00	4,182.00	4,258.00	4,336.00	4,415.00

Source: United Nations

67

Western Europe accounts for 60% of all world tourist arrivals, and 55% of all nights. The share held by Western Europe has dipped slightly over recent years due to an increase in tourist travel to developing regions, but the decline has been by no means a sharp one. The average length of stay in Western Europe is slightly above the average for the world at six days per visit.

Two regions take second position in terms of total tourist arrivals each with a 14% share. Perhaps surprisingly, one of these is Eastern Europe; 47 million people travelled to countries there in 1980. Less surprisingly, the second is the North and Central American region U.S.A., Canada, Mexico and the Caribbean countries. And as stays here were longer than in Eastern Europe this region moves well ahead in terms of the number of nights spent in the country. By this criteria, Eastern Europe, which has a very brief average length of stay, slips back into fourth position out of the eight regions, although the differences in compiling the figures should again be heeded.

The remaining five regions have only one-eighth of the total world consumption of tourists, although it is here that most of the growth has occurred. The Far East had a 4.8% share in 1980 compared with 3.4% in 1975, and South America has also shown a proportional increase. Although only accounting for 1.7% of world tourist consumption, Oceania has the longest length of stay, with an average of 14 days, and therefore figures more prominently in terms of nights spent. It has a 5% market share on this basis.

Table 54.   World Tourist Consumption by Region

('000s)	1975	1976	1977	1978	1979	1980
West Europe	175.1	181.7	191.5	193.4	210.0	215.1
East Europe	37.6	39.1	42.4	47.6	47.6	47.4
North and Central America	39.9	41.2	42.4	44.4	45.2	47.9
South America	4.5	4.7	5.2	5.8	6.8	7.1
North Africa and Middle East	8.0	8.4	9.8	9.2	9.6	9.7
Africa	3.6	4.0	4.1	4.4	4.8	5.2
Far East	9.4	10.4	12.2	14.2	15.0	16.6
Oceania	4.0	4.5	4.7	5.2	5.7	6.2
Total	282.1	294.0	312.2	324.2	344.6	355.2

Source: Own Calculations

Table 55.   Total Tourist Nights by Region

	1975	1976	1977	1978	1979	1980
Western Europe(1)	793.6	804.5	831.9	863.5	911.5	922.7
Eastern Europe(1)	63.6	59.8	59.6	70.7	74.7	76.2
North and Central America	336.7	359.9	362.3	398.2	407.8	419.9
South America	21.6	23.6	24.5	26.4	29.1	30.1
North Africa and Middle East	35.2	39.7	45.8	42.0	45.7	46.1
Africa	15.6	17.2	18.6	20.1	21.5	22.9
Far East	47.1	52.7	60.2	68.9	73.6	79.8
Oceania	53.5	60.5	62.5	69.3	79.7	88.7
Total	1,366.9	1,417.9	1,465.4	1,559.1	1,643.4	1,686.3

Source: Own Calculations
Note: (1) In registered accommodation

Table 56.   Average Length of Stay by Region

	1975	1976	1977	1978	1979	1980
Western Europe	6.3	6.3	6.3	6.1	6.1	6.2
Eastern Europe	4.7	4.6	4.5	4.6	4.8	4.8
North and Central America	8.4	8.7	8.5	9.0	9.0	8.8
South America	4.8	5.0	4.7	4.5	4.3	4.2
North Africa and Middle East	4.4	4.7	4.7	4.6	4.8	4.8
Africa	4.2	4.2	4.4	4.5	4.3	4.3
Far East	5.0	5.1	4.9	4.9	4.9	4.8
Oceania	13.4	13.6	13.2	13.4	14.1	14.3
Overall Average	4.8	4.8	4.7	4.8	4.8	4.7

Source: Own Calculations based on W.T.O., O.E.C.D. and national sources in many
            countries.
Note: Figures calculated by dividing the number of tourist nights by the number of
visits. Figures for **Europe** are based on dividing the number of arrivals at registered
accommodation into the total number of nights in registered accommodation, but the
overall average is **all** tourist arrivals divided into **all** tourist nights.

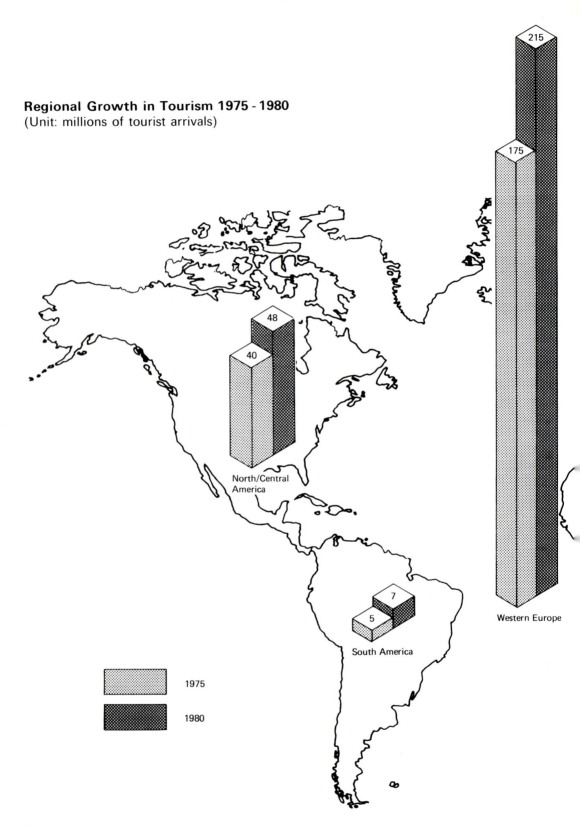

Regional Growth in Tourism 1975 - 1980
(Unit: millions of tourist arrivals)

215

175

48

40

North/Central
America

7

5

South America

Western Europe

1975

1980

Eastern Europe
47
38

North Africa/
Middle East
10
8

Far East
17
9

Africa
5
4

Oceania
6
4

Regional Population and Tourist Consumption 1980 (1975 = 100)

120
109
North/Central
America

12
103
Western Eu

140
114
South America

POPULATION

TOURIST CONSUMPTION

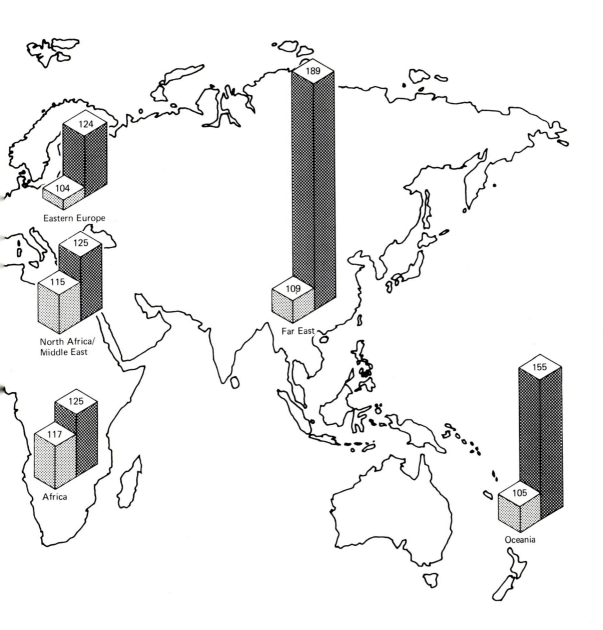

Eastern Europe

124

104

North Africa/
Middle East

125

115

Africa

125

117

Far East

189

109

Oceania

155

105

73

1.   Western Europe

We have seen that Western Europe is the world's primary tourist destination with well over half the cake. It receives a large number of tourist travellers from within its region, and from major travelling nations throughout the world.

The most notable increases in tourist arrivals in Western Europe were in 1976 (+ 5%) and in 1979 (+ 9%). Overall the growth rate has been about 3.5% per annum, but in 1980, an increase of only 2% occurred.

Several European countries contest leadership of the Western European market. In terms of total tourist arrivals at frontiers, Spain leads with a 17% market share, ahead of France (14%), Austria (13%), West Germany (12%) and Italy (11%). The only other country to have more than 10 million tourists in 1980 was the United Kingdom, which only had a 6% share on this basis.

The growth in tourism has mainly been in southern Europe; Spain, Portugal, Greece, Italy and Cyprus have all shown distinct growth, ahead of that in the north west. This is indicative of an increase in holiday traffic.

In terms of arrivals in tourist accommodation, France comes out on top with a 20% share, ahead of Spain with 15%. On this basis, Italy comes up into third position behind these two, arrivals at accommodation in Italy rose to 13% of the total in 1980 against 11% in 1975. And Italy goes ahead of Spain into second place behind France in terms of tourist arrivals at hotels, where the shares were 18.5% for France, 14% for Italy and only 10% for Spain. This stresses the importance of supplementary accommodation in Spain.

The picture is rather different when we come to look at tourist nights. France has surprising dominance here due to a lengthy average staying period of nine days; 25% of tourist nights in 1980 were in France. If we look at nights, the position of the United Kingdom is much improved; the average length of stay here is 14 days — one of the highest in Europe. This boosts the U.K.'s market share to 16% on this basis and into third position behind France and Spain. But the shares held by all these have fallen, with increases in nights spent in Greece, Portugal and Italy.

Although 1980 was not a good year for this region, 1981 was better and Europe has on the whole successfully retained its leading world position amidst difficulties. The recession, rising costs, and the high price of air travel have all created problems for the region, and the Europeans have had to fight hard to overcome the competition, particularly from North America where the low dollar has been a massive incentive. But if a levelling of growth would seem inevitable, Western Europe still has attractions which are unique, and sightseeing remains a strong factor on the holiday side. As its commercial draw is indisputable, business visitors are likely to be a growth area, and visits to and from friends and relatives will continue to play their role.

Spain had a particularly poor year in 1980, a result of inflation, bad publicity over hotel accommodation, and the ETA bombing campaigns. The depreciation of the peseta may help the financial aspects, but Spain may well start to lose out to smaller countries such as neighbouring Portugal where the stability since the 1974 revolution and a considerable amount of tourist investment has helped to attract a growing number of visitors.

The United Kingdom has had a marked levelling in tourist intake following several years of growth, partly as a result of rising prices and dissatisfaction with accommodation. As even the Royal Wedding in 1981 failed to stimulate tourism as anticipated, the travel industry had to counter the adverse publicity of the Summer riots. As we discussed in Chapter Two, political and social distrubances are bad news for the travel market wherever they occur, and this is further emphasised in the decline in tourist visits to Ireland.

The natural disasters in Italy took their toll, too, although Italy's long term prospects are good. The country draws many tourists from within Europe, and has been less susceptible than some to the fall in American intake. France, too, has held up well; in fact their tourist market is about the best in Europe at present, with full bookings in the industry, and no marked political effects.

Switzerland and Austria continue to do well from tourism, although weather conditions in 1980 were a problem. The countries benefit from their joint summer/winter attractions, and draw many road visitors from their large neighbours. Price has been the main problem here, with Italy a less expensive alternative, close at hand.

West Germany is enjoying mixed fortunes, benefiting more from casual stays rather than long-term, and the Scandinavian area is stable but not showing any pronounced growth.

2.   Eastern Europe

We have noted that Eastern Europe receives a sizeable number of tourist visitors, but the length of stay is brief and the world share of tourist nights is much lower.

There have been considerable fluctuations in recent years in the shares of tourist traffic held by Eastern European countries. Czechoslovakia, for example, had an 18% market share in 1975, but only 8% in 1980; while the USSR, Hungary and Romania have shown notable increases. The leading country in terms of both tourist arrivals at frontiers and at registered accommodation is Yugoslavia with about a 25% share overall.

In terms of nights spent in Eastern Europe (in registered accommodation), there have been less fluctuations in the trends. On this basis, Yugoslavia has a one-third market share, well ahead of the USSR and Bulgaria in second and third place.

Yugoslavia is the main country to benefit from holiday travel, and may have suffered from the uncertain political climate following Tito's death. The political environment in the other Eastern European countries is scarcely an attraction for tourists, least so in Poland where a slump is inevitable.

3.   North and Central America

48 million people travelled to and within North and Central America in 1980 compared with under 40 million in 1975. But the rate of growth has been under 3% per annum, and was certainly slower than many regions until the healthy 6% increase in 1980.

Of the tourist arrivals in 1980, almost 47% went to the U.S.A., and the proportion has been steadily on the increase. In 1980, in fact, increases in visits to America accounted for 90% of the total increases for the region, so we can see that the trend in the other countries has been bleak, with little or no growth. Certainly the fortunes of the Caribbean have been mixed, while Mexico's growth has been halted by inflation, but the sharpest fall has been in travel to Canada, which had one-third of the region's consumption in 1975, only one-quarter in 1980.

Some of the smaller countries in this region have considerably more tourist visitors than they have inhabitants. The Bahamas, with a population of a quarter of a million, had 1.2 million tourists in 1980; Bermuda's half a million visitors descended on a population of 60,000. They are countries which have developed their economies around the tourist industry. But their market shares in the region are small; most have under 1% of the total consumption, and only three countries (U.S.A., Canada, Mexico) have more than 5% of the market.

Average lengths of stay are fairly lengthy in this region, particularly in U.S.A. Here, the average tourist visit is 12 days, the longest in the region, and this extends the country's dominance of tourism in the region. In terms of nights spent in North and Central America, the U.S.A. accounts for two-thirds, well ahead of Canada (17%) and Mexico (10%).

The weak U.S. dollar has proved to be the strength of the U.S. travel market over the last two years, with a rising number of Europeans travelling to the States for holidays. Traditionally popular locations such as the West Coast and New York are being joined by Florida and Texas as the main draws. Seen by some as "a golden decade for tourism" the continued success of the U.S.A. as a tourist draw may now be hit by a stronger currency and air travel increases in the aftermath of Laker. So the current rush to the States, which mirrors the rush to Spain in the 1960's, will probably not continue at the same rate for long.

Canada has not enjoyed the same success as the U.S.A. as yet, and the last two years have been less encouraging than the mid-70's trends. Facilities are somewhat restricted at present, and the country relies heavily on U.S. traffic which has slowed.

Mexico also has problems due to very high prices on all types of tourist services. The country is about 50% more expensive than the U.S.A.

The Caribbean has seen its tourist intake slow, and the region is troubled economically. Jamaica has been hit by numerous problems, and the arrivals to several islands are falling.

4.   South America

South America has only a small share of the world tourist market — under 2% — but is increasing fast. The overall growth rate between 1976 and 1980 was 50%, i.e. 10% per annum, although the 4% increase in 1980 was not impressive. Despite politcal troubles, the region is encouraging tourism and is a rapidly expanding market for business visitors.

South America received a total of 7 million tourist visitors in 1980. Four countries accounted for two-thirds of the total; the lead contested between Colombia and Uruguay, both with a 17% share. But these were short trips, Uruguay's average being only 1.4 nights, and a large number were overnight stays only. A breakdown by number of nights presents a very different picture with Brazil accounting for 30% of all nights spent in the region. Venezuela also rises to prominence on this basis with a 23% share, both countries had average stays of eight days, the highest in the region.

5.   North Africa and the Middle East

Despite the obvious business interest in the Middle East, and the holiday potential of the North African coast, tourist visits to this region have shown sluggish growth. The rise from 8 million tourists in 1975 to 9.6 million in 1980 averages at only 4% per annum, certainly much slower than the average for the developing regions.

An analysis by country reveals that the region has held up better in its holiday resorts. Holiday orientated markets such as Israel, Jordan and Tunisia have shown marked growth, although neither Morocco nor Algeria have matched this. Declines have occurred in visits to Iran, Saudi Arabia, Libya, Lebanon and Syria, and we can see the impact of political strife in some of these countries.

The largest markets in the region are Morocco, which has retained a static share, and Tunisia which has grown. But the most distinct growth has occurred in Jordan; it held only a 9% market share in 1975 rising to 12% in 1980. Israel is well down the list, although it is by far the largest market for tourists outside of the Middle East region.

Both Jordan and Tunisia have lengthy average stays of over seven days, so their importance increases if we look at tourist consumption in terms of number of nights. On this bais, Tunisia has 25% of the market, and Jordan, 20%. The latter has shown considerable growth in this respect, as has Israel.

The considerable amount of business intake in the Middle East has led to a vast increase in hotel accommodation and travel facilities, and the area has become a popular conference centre. But the rate of influx is below expectation and this has resulted in low occupancy rates.

Israel's high rate of inflation has not posed problems for the travel industry as the currency is deflated against foreign currencies. Prospects partly depend on political factors; tourism rose fast after the peace treaty with Egypt.

6.   Africa

Under 2% of the world's tourists travel to African countries, and the annual growth rate of 6% per annum has been steady rather than striking for a potentially expansive area. Although many African countries have committed themselves to tourist expansion, the results have been slow coming, and the development projects have been indered by organisational problems and shortage of cash.

Amidst a large number of countries, with small shares of the total regional intake, two countries stand out — Egypt and South Africa. They have 40% of the total tourist arrivals in the region, well ahead of Kenya and Tanzania with 7.5% and 6% respective shares. The other countries, including such tourist centres as The Seychelles have small shares of the market.

Egypt has developed its dominance from a 20% share in 1975 to 25% in 1980. Other countries to show above average growth include Botswana, taking almost 5% in 1980, Mauritius and Upper Volta.

The average length of stay among African countries varies considerably; it is over 11 days in The Gambia and Mauritius, only just over one night in Angola, Botswana and Lesotho, and this has a considerable effect on the structure of the market in terms of nights. On this basis, Egypt has a one-third share of the market, while Kenya accounts for a 15% share.

7. Far East

Travel to and within the Far East region has risen rapidly in recent years. Tourist arrivals increased by 12% per annum between 1975 and 1980 to reach a 5% share of the world traffic. Growth was particularly strident in 1980, when amidst a general slowing in the rate of increase, tourist visits to the Far East rose by over 10%.

Only three countries among the many in the area accounted for over 10% of tourist arrivals; they were Hong Kong, Singapore and Thailand. But lengths of stay vary considerably, and the picture is rather different in terms of nights spent in this region. The above countries have shortish stays, often being used merely as overnight stops, while other countries have long stays and are consequently much more important on the basis of nights stayed. A good case in point is India, where the average length of stay is 25 days, bringing the market share in terms of nights to 25%.

There have been notable increases in this region in the Philippines, Singapore, Sri Lanka and China in terms of tourist visits.

8. Oceania

The Oceanic region receives almost as many tourist visitors as the Far East, over 6 million in 1980. Despite the inclusion of Australia and New Zealand, 70% of total tourist arrivals in this region are to one country — Hawaii, which also accounted for 50% of all nights.

The Oceanic region includes a number of tourist islands, but they have a small intake of tourists in terms of the total for the region. Apart from the three named above, only Fiji has more than a 1% market share.

Lengths of stay in this region are the longest in the world. The average for the region is 14 days, and this rises to 16 days in New Zealand and 36 days in Australia. As a result, an evaluation by nights gives Australia a larger market share, 37% against 50% for Hawaii.

The region as a whole has shown pronounced growth, since 1976 about 8% per annum. Growth in 1980 was close to 10%. Hawaii has continued to do well, as have some of the small islands such as Vanuatu, the Solomon Islands and Fiji. In these areas, tourist arrivals have more or less doubled over the last five years.

Oceania should do well in the future; as more people travel, they reach further and further, and islands such as Hawaii have considerable allure in Europe but few people have so far visited them.

Table 57.   TOTAL POPULATION 1976-1980

Region 1 : Western Europe

Millions	1976	1977	1978	1979	1980
Andorra	0.03	0.03	0.03	0.03	0.03
Austria	7.51	7.52	7.51	7.51	7.51
Belgium	9.82	9.83	9.84	9.85	9.86
Cyprus	0.61	0.61	0.62	0.62	0.63
Denmark	5.07	5.09	5.10	5.12	5.12
Finland	4.73	4.74	4.75	4.76	4.78
France	52.89	53.08	53.28	53.48	53.71
Germany, West	61.51	61.40	61.31	61.44	61.56
Gibraltar	0.03	0.03	0.03	0.03	0.03
Greece	9.17	9.27	9.36	9.45	9.60
Iceland	0.22	0.22	0.22	0.23	0.23
Ireland	3.23	3.27	3.31	3.37	3.40
Italy	56.17	56.46	56.71	56.91	57.04
Jersey	0.06	0.07	0.07	0.07	0.07
Liechtenstein	0.02	0.02	0.03	0.03	0.03
Luxembourg	0.36	0.36	0.36	0.36	0.36
Malta	0.33	0.33	0.34	0.35	0.36
Monaco	0.03	0.03	0.03	0.03	0.03
Netherlands	13.77	13.85	13.94	14.03	14.14
Norway	4.03	4.04	4.06	4.07	4.09
Portugal	9.67	9.74	9.80	9.84	9.93
San Marino	0.02	0.02	0.02	0.02	0.02
Spain	35.97	36.35	36.78	37.18	37.43
Sweden	8.22	8.25	8.28	8.29	8.31
Switzerland	6.35	6.33	6.34	6.36	6.37
Turkey	41.04	42.08	43.14	44.24	44.92
United Kingdom	55.89	55.85	55.84	55.88	55.95
TOTAL	386.75	388.87	391.10	393.55	395.54

Source: United Nations.

Table 58.   TOURIST ARRIVALS AT FRONTIERS

Region 1 : Western Europe

'000	1975	1976	1977	1978	1979	1980
Andorra	6,059	6,450	6,700	6,900	7,000	7,250
Austria	25,000	23,500	24,000	26,000	27,000	28,400
Belgium	5,000	5,000	5,000	4,800	4,800	5,000
Cyprus	47	180	178	217	297	360
Denmark	3,500	3,700	3,700	3,600	3,600	3,500
Finland	2,600	3,000	3,500	3,600	4,000	4,150
France	24,000	25,036	26,265	27,300	28,763	30,100
Germany (W)	25,000	27,500	25,000	25,000	25,500	26,000
Gibraltar	125	120	115	110	135	139
Greece	2,840	3,672	3,961	4,532	5,233	4,796
Iceland	72	70	73	76	77	66
Ireland	1,688	1,690	1,963	2,257	2,250	2,200
Italy	15,050	16,207	18,657	19,352	21,919	22,600
Jersey	775	780	784	790	800	840
Liechtenstein	75	77	80	73	70	73
Luxembourg	1,250	1,250	1,200	1,200	1,250	1,250
Malta	335	340	366	484	618	747
Monaco	300	400	450	460	475	480
Netherlands	4,500	4,750	4,800	4,800	5,000	5,200
Norway	3,000	3,000	3,200	3,500	3,600	3,700
Portugal	889	958	1,369	1,681	2,251	2,708
San Marino	2,426	2,436	2,565	2,955	3,000	3,100
Spain	30,122	30,014	33,854	29,970	38,902	38,027
Turkey	1,201	1,336	1,259	1,428	1,524	1,288
United Kingdom	9,490	10,808	12,281	12,646	12,493	12,393
Sweden	1,750	1,778	1,800	1,800	1,800	1,850
Switzerland	8,040	7,609	8,341	7,855	7,608	8,873
TOTAL	175,134	181,661	191,461	193,386	209,965	215,090

Source: National Statistical Offices/National Tourist Offices/WTO/OECD/Own Estimates.

Table 59. TOURIST ARRIVALS AT REGISTERED ACCOMMODATION

Region 1 : Western Europe

'000	1975	1976	1977	1978	1979	1980
Andorra	20	20	22	23	25	26
Austria	11,540	11,598	11,748	12,254	12,875	13,879
Belgium	4,000	4,000	3,800	3,500	3,400	3,600
Cyprus	45	128	126	166	234	254
Denmark	3,140	3,230	3,400	3,350	3,250	3,200
Finland	1,750	1,800	1,800	1,750	1,800	1,800
France	24,500	25,036	25,905	26,846	28,000	28,100
Germany (W)	8,810	9,356	10,000	9,500	8,940	9,706
Gibraltar	110	108	105	100	125	130
Greece	3,574	4,850	5,049	5,773	6,428	5,850
Iceland	66	64	66	69	70	68
Ireland	1,289	1,278	1,470	1,690	1,676	1,650
Italy	13,234	13,930	14,836	15,321	17,699	18,137
Jersey	760	765	775	790	800	810
Liechtenstein	30	30	35	30	30	30
Luxembourg	600	600	565	560	525	530
Malta	333	336	356	473	614	675
Monaco	150	200	225	230	236	240
Netherlands	3,648	3,848	3,866	3,900	4,000	4,100
Norway	2,800	2,950	2,750	2,700	2,800	2,800
Portugal	836	841	1,479	1,733	2,063	2,283
San Marino	50	50	50	50	50	52
Spain	17,000	15,300	14,406	21,000	22,000	21,800
Sweden	1,750	1,778	1,800	1,800	1,800	1,850
Switzerland	8,040	7,609	8,341	7,855	7,608	8,873
Turkey	520	560	531	670	598	413
United Kingdom	7,972	9,036	10,118	10,363	10,189	10,200
TOTAL	116,567	119,301	123,624	127,320	137,835	141,056

Source: National Statistical Offices/National Tourist Offices/WTO/OECD/Own Estimates.

Table 60.   TOURIST NIGHTS IN REGISTERED ACCOMMODATION

Region 1 : Western Europe

'000	1975	1976	1977	1978	1979	1980
Andorra	50	50	55	58	62	68
Austria	79,938	79,051	78,378	81,241	84,825	90,203
Belgium	8,040	7,914	7,623	7,029	6,829	7,250
Cyprus	169	588	729	1,026	1,578	2,200
Denmark	7,536	8,534	8,514	8,410	8,299	8,226
Finland	2,750	2,525	2,600	2,500	2,700	2,980
France	205,000	215,000	218,000	225,000	230,000	235,000
W. Germany	19,899	21,621	18,775	19,814	20,814	22,724
Gibraltar	750	755	735	700	750	755e
Greece	14,812	20,826	20,239	24,356	28,827	26,300e
Iceland	450	450	460	480	540	520e
Ireland	17,402	17,415	19,245	21,485	21,118	21,300e
Italy	73,981	75,299	81,095	87,552	101,978	103,265
Jersey	4,450	4,600	4,890	6,251	7,000	8,000e
Liechtenstein	60	60	60	60	60	62
Luxembourg	1,200	1,200	1,125	1,120	1,050	1,200e
Malta	4,633	4,804	4,841	6,484	8,359	10,300e
Monaco	525	730	750	775	780	820e
Netherlands	11,845	12,095	11,548	10,201	10,455	11,000e
Norway	5,594	5,881	5,527	5,503	5,398	5,898
Portugal	3,750	4,000	6,838	7,768	9,215	10,139
San Marino	70	70	70	70	70	72
Spain	165,710	151,486	154,000	160,000	170,000	168,000
Sweden	2,900	2,900	2,946	3,196	3,360	3,195
Switzerland	32,258	31,063	32,942	31,471	30,314	36,026
Turkey	1,300	1,400	1,366	1,841	1,631	1,114
United Kingdom	128,500	134,200	148,500	149,100	155,500	146,100
TOTAL	793,572	804,517	831,924	863,491	911,522	922,717

Source: National Statistical Offices/National Tourist Offices/WTO/OECD/Own Estimates.

Table 61. AVERAGE LENGTH OF STAY — ALL REGISTERED ACCOMMODATION

Region 1 : Western Europe

(days)	1975	1976	1977	1978	1979	1980
Andorra	2.5	2.5	2.5	2.5	2.5	2.6
Austria	6.9	6.8	6.7	6.6	6.6	6.4
Belgium	2.0	2.0	2.0	2.0	2.0	2.2
Cyprus	3.8	4.6	5.8	6.2	6.7	8.7
Denmark	2.4	2.6	2.5	2.5	2.5	2.6
Finland	1.6	1.4	1.4	1.4	1.5	1.7
France	9.3	9.4	9.4	9.1	9.0	8.7
W. Germany	2.3	2.3	1.8	1.9	2.0	2.2
Gibraltar	6.8	7.0	7.0	7.0	6.0	5.8
Greece	4.1	4.3	4.0	4.2	4.5	4.5
Iceland	6.8	7.0	7.0	7.0	7.7	7.6
Ireland	13.5	13.6	13.1	12.7	12.6	12.9
Jersey	3.5	6.0	6.3	7.9	8.8	9.9
Liechtenstein	2.0	2.0	1.7	2.0	2.0	2.1
Luxembourg	2.0	2.0	2.0	2.0	2.0	2.3
Malta	13.9	14.3	13.6	13.7	13.6	15.3
Monaco	3.5	3.7	3.3	3.4	3.3	3.4
Netherlands	3.2	3.1	3.0	2.6	2.6	2.7
Norway	2.0	2.0	2.0	2.0	1.9	2.1
Portugal	4.5	4.8	4.6	4.5	4.5	4 4
San Marino	1.4	1.4	1.4	1.4	1.4	1.4
Sweden	1.7	1.6	1.6	1.8	1.9	1.7
Switzerland	4.0	4.1	3.9	4.0	4.0	4.1
Turkey	2.5	2.5	2.6	2.7	2.7	2.7
United Kingdom	16.1	14.9	14.7	14.4	15.3	14.3
TOTAL	6.8	6.8	6.7	6.8	6.6	6.5

Source: National Statistical Offices/National Tourist Offices/WTO/OECD/Own Estimates.

Table 62. **TOURIST ARRIVALS AT HOTELS**

Region 1 : Western Europe

'000	1975	1976	1977	1978	1979	1980
Andorra	10	10	10	11	11	11e
Austria	7,677	7,836	8,090	8,476	8,935	9,685
Belgium	2,500	2,400	2,440	2,250	2,200	2.250e
Cyprus	38	105	122	157	166	170e
Denmark	7,536	8,534	8,514	8,410	8,299	7,856
Finland	400	400	375	400	450	460e
France	16,773	17,385	17,700e	18,250	19,000	19,100e
W. Germany	6,902	7,337	7,832	8,011	8,271	8,400e
Gibraltar	40	29	25	31	35	37e
Greece	3,239	4,850	4,869	5,120	5,717	5,300e
Iceland	35	36	38	40	42	40
Ireland	482	530	566	640	625	620e
Italy	10,797	11,501	12,281	12,583	14,333	14,616
Jersey	575	580	575	613	625	630e
Liechtenstein	15	15	18	15	15	16e
Luxembourg	500	497	471	465	438	440e
Malta	186	181	197	255	322	360e
Monaco	139	181	209	215	220	225e
Netherlands	2,742	2,910	2,788	2,683	2,750	2,960e
Norway	1,126	1,191	1,238	1,233	1,252	1,252
Portugal	708	728	1,228	1,437	1,693	1,802
San Marino	40	40	40	40	40	42e
Spain	11,984	10,474	13,761	12,177	10,370	10,320e
Sweden	1,550	1,595	1,600	1,600	1,650	1,700e
Switzerland	6,199	5,879	6,502	6,033	5,798	6,661
Turkey	350	375	350	450	400	360e
United Kingdom	6,000	6,800	7,600	7,800	7,650	7,620e
TOTAL	88,543	92,399	99,439	99,395	101,307	103,377

Source: National Statistical Offices/National Tourist Offices/WTO/OECD/Own Estimates.

Table 63. TOURIST NIGHTS IN HOTELS

Region 1 : Western Europe

'000	1975	1976	1977	1978	1979	1980
Andorra e	25	25	25	30	30	32e
Austria	46,046	46,762	47,346	49,561	52,079	55,578
Belgium	4,669	4,551	4,629	4,280	4,268	4,349
Cyprus	167	579	678	931	1,370	1,800e
Denmark	3,692	3,967	4,176	4,277	4,257	4,349
Finland	1,647	1,514	1,486	1,586	1,723	1,843
France	100,015	103,126	107,000	108,000	111,000	114,500e
W. Germany	13,658	14,703	15,669	16,248	17,136	18,000e
Gibraltar	260	216	175	219	239	242e
Greece	13,444	18,675	18,162	21,877	26,172	25,100e
Iceland	245	250	260	280	325	300e
Ireland	2,750	3,002	2,813	3,182	3,000	2,900e
Italy	47,529	49,557	54,040	56,936	66,285	66,396
Jersey	3,300	3,350	3,450	3,700	4,000	4,400e
Liechtenstein	30	30	30	30	30	32e
Luxembourg	950	950	930	919	885	950e
Malta	2,091	1,929	2,054	2,811	3,580	4,300e
Monaco	489	695	700	725	730	760e
Netherlands	6,612	6,028	6,062	5,752	6,041	6,300e
Norway	2,387	2,493	2,438	2,348	2,361	2,430
Portugal	3,328	2,626	6,167	6,796	7,835	8,230
San Marino	58	61	59	62	60	62e
Spain	65,710	56,486	72,969	82,500	86,000	85,000e
Sweden	2,450	2,500	2,500	2,507	2,809	2,659
Switzerland	18,987	18,047	19,393	18,496	16,924	19,980
Turkey	845	900	890	1,200	1,060	990
United Kingdom	96,000	100,000	110,000	112,000	116,000	115,500e
TOTAL	437,384	443,022	484,101	507,253	536,199	546,833

Source: National Statistical Offices/National Tourist Offices/WTO/OECD/Own Estimates.

Table 64.   **TOTAL POPULATION 1975-1980**

Region 2 : Eastern Europe

Millions	1975	1976	1977	1978	1979	1980
Albania	2.42	2.48	2.55	2.61	2.67	2.73
Bulgaria	8.72	8.76	8.80	8.81	8.95	8.86
Czechoslovakia	14.80	14.92	15.03	15.14	15.25	15.32
East Germany	16.85	16.79	16.77	16.76	16.74	16.74
Hungary	10.54	10.60	10.65	10.68	10.70	10.71
Poland	34.02	34.36	34.70	35.01	35.26	35.58
Romania	21.25	21.45	21.66	21.85	22.05	22.27
USSR	254.47	256.76	259.03	261.25	263.42	265.54
Yugoslavia	21.37	21.57	21.78	21.97	22.16	22.34
TOTAL	384.44	387.69	390.97	394.08	397.20	400.09

Source: United Nations.

Table 65. TOURIST ARRIVALS AT FRONTIERS

Region 2 : Eastern Europe

'000	1975	1976	1977	1978	1979	1980
Albania	25	25	30	30	35	32
Bulgaria	2,092	2,070	2,390	2,904	3,100	3,000
Czechoslovakia	6,900	6,952	6,821	4,682	3,984	4,000
E. Germany	3,000	3,000	3,000	3,500	3,600	3,750
Hungary	4,995	5,551	7,183	9,950	9,847	9,450
Poland	3,664	4,429	4,850	5,000	5,000	4,600
Romania	3,206	3,169	3,685	5,018	5,250	5,300
USSR	3,691	3,879	4,400	5,500	6,000	6,300
Yugoslavia	10,000	10,000	10,000	11,000	10,800	11,000
TOTAL	37,573	39,075	42,359	47,584	47,616	47,432

Source: National Statistical Offices/National Tourist Offices/WTO/OECD/Own Estimates.

Table 66. TOURIST ARRIVALS IN ALL REGISTERED ACCOMMODATION

Region 2 : Eastern Europe

'000	1975	1976	1977	1978	1979	1980
Albania	9	10	10	11	11	10
Bulgaria	1,690	1,500	1,500	1,680	1,725	1,700
Czechoslovakia	2,700	2,700	2,696	2,949	3,108	3,200
E. Germany	1,407	1,413	1,425	1,420	1,509	1,500
Hungary	2,143	2,195	2,357	2,947	2,829	2,800
Poland	1,780	1,832	1,865	2,135	2,111	1,800
Romania	2,114	1,890	1,737	2,251	2,411	2,460
USSR	2,500	2,500	2,850	3,600	3,900	4,000
Yugoslavia	5,835	5,572	5,621	6,384	5,966	6,410
TOTAL	20,178	19,612	20,061	23,377	23,570	23,880

Source: National Statistical Offices/National Tourist Offices/WTO/OECD/Own Estimates.

Table 67.   TOURIST NIGHTS IN ALL ACCOMMODATION

Region 2 : Eastern Europe

'000	1975	1976	1977	1978	1979	1980
Albania	45	50	50	55	55	50
Bulgaria	15,855	14,279	14,287	15,958	16,824	16,700
Czechoslovakia	7,250	7,300	7,342	8,150	9,628	9,500
E. Germany	4,030	4,050	4,100	4,095	4,048	4,100
Hungary	7,412	7,666	8,587	11,046	11,272	11,000
Poland	6,200	6,331	6,189	6,823	6,919	6,500
Romania	9,681	7,500	6,498	8,642	10,189	10,200
USSR	13,000	13,000	15,000	19,000	20,000	20,500
Yugoslavia	31,622	29,368	29,026	34,866	33,482	36,978
TOTAL	95,095	89,644	91,079	108,635	112,417	115,528

Source: National Statistical Offices/National Tourist Offices/WTO/OECD/Own Estimates.

Table 68.   AVERAGE LENGTH OF STAY

Region 2 : Eastern Europe

(days)	1975	1976	1977	1978	1979	1980
Albania	5.0	5.0	5.0	5.0	5.0	5.0
Bulgaria	9.4	9.5	9.5	9.5	9.7	9.8
Czechoslovakia	2.7	2.7	2.7	2.8	3.1	3.0
East Germany	2.9	2.9	2.9	2.7	2.7	2.7
Hungary	3.5	3.5	3.6	3.7	4.0	3.9
Poland	3.5	3.5	3.3	3.2	3.3	2.6
Romania	4.6	4.0	3.7	3.8	4.2	4.2
USSR	5.2	5.2	5.3	5.3	5.2	5.1
Yugoslavia	5.4	5.3	5.2	5.5	5.6	5.8
TOTAL	4.7	4.6	4.5	4.6	4.8	4.8

Source: National Statistical Offices/National Tourist Offices/WTO/OECD/Own Estimates.

Table 69.　　　　　　　　TOURIST ARRIVALS AT HOTELS

Region 2 : Eastern Europe

'000	1975	1976	1977	1978	1979	1980
Albania	7	8	8	9	9	8
Bulgaria	1,130	985	950	1,025	1,035	1,000
Czechoslovakia	2,000	2,000	2,037	2,123	2,251	2,200
E. Germany	1,084	1,085	1,057	1,052	1,080	1,120
Hungary	1,250	1,280	1,322	1,626	1,584	1,550
Poland	1,679	1,739	1,343	1,638	1,617	1,500
Romania	1,761	1,607	1,428	1,876	2,173	2,200
USSR	2,250	2,250	2,600	3,300	3,500	3,700
Yugoslavia	3,860	3,710	3,679	4,156	3,900	4,000
TOTAL	15,021	14,664	14,424	16,805	17,149	17,278

Source: National Statistical Offices/National Tourist Offices/WTO/OECD/Own Estimates.

Table 70.　　　　　　　　TOURIST NIGHTS IN HOTELS

Region 2 : Eastern Europe

'000	1975	1976	1977	1978	1979	1980
Albania	35	40	40	45	45	44
Bulgaria	10,714	9,358	8,890	9,778	11,076	11,000
Czechoslovakia	5,000	5,000	5,088	5,520	5,985	5,900
E. Germany	2,796	2,709	2,860	2,899	2,950	3,010
Hungary	3,235	3,141	3,385	4,093	4,130	4,050
Poland	3,512	3,703	3,698	4,432	4,481	4,200
Romania	8,102	6,433	5,374	7,110	9,407	9,500
USSR	11,250	11,500	13,000	16,000	17,500	18,000
Yugoslavia	18,924	17,930	17,277	20,844	19,000	20,527
TOTAL	63,568	59,814	59,612	70,721	74,574	76,231

Source: National Statistical Offices/National Tourist Offices/WTO/OECD/Own Estimates.

Table 71. TOTAL POPULATION 1975-1980

Region 3 : North & Central America

Millions	1975	1976	1977	1978	1979	1980
Antigua	0.07	0.07	0.07	0.07	0.08	0.08
Aruba	0.01	0.01	0.01	0.01	0.01	0.01
Bahamas	0.20	0.21	0.22	0.23	0.22	0.24
Barbados	0.24	0.25	0.25	0.27	0.25	0.25
Belize	0.14	0.14	0.15	0.15	0.16	0.16
Bermuda	0.06	0.06	0.06	0.06	0.06	0.06
Bonaire	0.01	0.01	0.01	0.01	0.01	0.01
British Virgin Isles	0.01	0.01	0.01	0.01	0.01	0.01
Canada	22.73	23.02	23.26	23.49	23.69	23.94
Costa Rica	1.96	2.01	2.07	2.12	2.17	2.24
Cuba	9.33	9.46	9.60	9.69	9.77	9.83
Grenada	0.11	0.11	0.11	0.11	0.11	0.10
Guadeloupe	0.33	0.33	0.32	0.32	0.32	0.33
Guatemala	6.24	6.43	6.63	6.84	7.05	7.26
Haiti	4.58	4.67	4.75	4.83	4.92	5.01
Honduras	3.09	3.20	3.32	3.44	3.56	3.69
Jamaica	2.04	2.07	2.10	2.12	2.16	2.19
Martinique	0.32	0.32	0.32	0.33	0.32	0.33
Mexico	60.15	62.33	64.59	66.94	69.38	71.91
Montserrat	0.01	0.01	0.01	0.01	0.01	0.01
Netherlands Antilles	0.24	0.25	0.25	0.25	0.26	0.27
Nicaragua	2.16	2.24	2.32	2.41	2.64	2.70
Panama	1.62	1.66	1.70	1.75	1.79	1.84
Puerto Rico	3.12	3.21	3.32	3.36	3.41	3.44
St. Kitts	0.07	0.07	0.07	0.07	0.07	0.07
St. Vincent	0.09	0.09	0.10	0.10	0.10	0.12
Trinidad & Tobago	1.08	1.10	1.12	1.13	1.13	1.14
U.S.A.	213.56	215.15	216.88	218.23	220.10	227.64
TOTAL	333.57	338.49	343.62	348.35	353.76	364.88

Source: United Nations.

Table 72.   TOURIST VISITS

Region 3 : North & Central America

'000	1975	1976	1977	1978	1979	1980
Antigua	63	57	68	77	88	87
Aruba	129	146	151	164	185	189
Bahamas	1,381	1,404	1,381	1,176	1,129	1,181
Barbados	222	224	269	316	371	369
Belize	50	55	59	60	62	62
Bermuda	412	450	439	420	459	492
Bonaire	18	18	19	20	20	23
British Virgin Isles	75	78	88	91	95	120
Canada	13,663	12,998	12,673	12,745	12,267	12,426
Cayman Isles	54	65	67	77	101	120
Costa Rica	297	300	328	340	350	355
Cuba	25	50	70	80	90	105
Curacao	241	318	309	304	286	301
Grenada	21	24	26	28	32	29
Guadeloupe	77	86	116	120	114	118
Guatemala	454	408	445	416	504	500
Haiti	77	86	95	112	118	140
Honduras	81	99	103	110	116	120
Jamaica	396	328	265	382	427	395
Martinique	105	120	135	148	159	158
Mexico	3,218	3,107	3,247	3,636	4,142	4,135
Montserrat	9	9	12	15	14	16
Netherlands Antilles	308	368	400	412	420	425
Nicaragua	189	207	212	218	225	220
Panama	283	314	363	390	386	380
Puerto Rico	1,339	1,300	1,358	1,474	1,714	1,697
St. Kitts	12	13	15	20	25	32
St. Vincent	32	35	37	29	33	38
Trinidad & Tobago	167	200	169	177	190	195
USA	15,698	17,523	18,610	19,842	20,016	22,500
Others	800	850	900	960	1,050	1,000
TOTAL	39,896	41,240	42,429	44,359	45,188	47,928

Source: National Statistical Offices/National Tourist Offices/WTO/OECD/Own Estimates.

Table 73.   TOURIST NIGHTS

Region 3 : North & Central America

'000	1975	1976	1977	1978	1979	1980
Antigua	300	300	320	350	380	375
Aruba	810	915	943	1,020	1,060	1,050
Bahamas	5,800	5,900	5,900	6,000	6,100	6,200
Barbados	1,120	1,274	1,470	1,725	1,900	1,900
Belize	175	200	200	200	220	225
Bermuda	1,900	2,100	2,050	2,000	2,340	2,500
Bonaire	60	60	65	65	70	75
British Virgin Isles	250	260	280	275	300	330
Canada	78,000	74,000	69,356	72,500	72,400	72,490
Cayman Isles	240	315	320	370	390	450
Costa Rica	640	660	1,027	704	710	720
Cuba	150	180	190	200	220	245
Curacao	600	660	570	650	650	655
Grenada	284	293	300	310	318	300
Guadeloupe	300	315	330	360	375	372
Guatemala	1,800	1,650	1,850	1,664	3,500	3,500
Haiti	192	218	236	264	280	315
Honduras	240	225	200	250	275	290
Jamaica	2,143	1,719	1,562	2,253	2,565	2,370
Martinique	470	540	610	650	680	680
Mexico	32,500	31,000	32,500	38,542	42,248	42,250
Montserrat	30	30	36	40	40	45
Netherlands Antilles	1,250	1,250	1,300	1,300	1,350	1,400
Nicaragua	890	900	850	880	900	900
Panama	693	754	825	915	996	990
Puerto Rico	1,378	1,270	1,474	1,662	1,700	1,680
St. Kitts	80	85	90	96	100	125
St. Vincent	110	120	125	150	160	175
Trinidad & Tobago	1,070	1,250	1,050	1,050	1,100	1,150
USA	200,000	228,000	232,622	258,000	260,250	272,000
Others	3,200	3,500	3,600	3,800	4,150	4,000
TOTAL	336,675	359,943	362,251	398,245	407,757	419,875

Source: National Statistical Offices/National Tourist Offices/WTO/OECD/Own Estimates.

Table 74. AVERAGE LENGTH OF STAY

Region 3 : North & Central America

Days	1975	1976	1977	1978	1979	1980
Antigua	4.8	5.3	4.7	4.5	4.3	4.3
Aruba	6.3	6.3	6.2	6.2	5.7	5.6
Bahamas	4.2	4.2	4.3	5.1	5.4	5.2
Barbados	5.0	5.7	5.5	5.5	5.1	5.1
Belize	3.5	3.6	3.4	3.3	3.5	3.5
Bermuda	4.6	4.7	4.7	4.8	5.1	5.3
Bonaire	3.3	3.3	3.4	3.3	3.5	3.3
British Virgin Isles	3.3	3.3	3.2	3.0	3.2	2.8
Canada	5.7	5.7	5.5	5.7	5.9	5.8
Cayman Isles	4.4	4.8	4.8	4.8	3.9	3.8
Costa Rica	2.2	2.2	3.1	2.1	2.0	2.0
Cuba	6.0	3.6	2.7	2.5	2.4	2.3
Dominican Rep.	2.5	2.1	1.8	2.1	2.3	2.2
Grenada	13.5	12.2	11.5	11.1	9.9	10.2
Guadeloupe	3.9	3.7	2.8	3.0	3.3	3.2
Guatemala	4.0	4.0	4.2	4.0	6.9	7.0
Haiti	2.5	2.5	2.5	2.4	2.4	2.3
Honduras	3.0	2.3	1.9	2.3	2.4	2.4
Jamaica	5.4	5.2	5.9	5.9	6.0	6.0
Martinique	4.5	4.5	4.5	4.4	4.3	4.3
Mexico	10.1	10.0	10.0	10.6	10.2	10.2
Montserrat	3.3	3.3	3.0	2.7	2.9	2.8
Netherlands Antilles	4.1	3.4	3.3	3.2	3.2	3.3
Nicaragua	4.7	4.4	4.0	4.0	4.0	4.1
Panama	2.4	2.4	2.3	2.3	2.6	2.6
Puerto Rico	1.0	1.0	1.0	1.0	1.0	1.0
St. Kitts	6.7	6.5	6.0	4.8	4.0	3.9
St. Vincent	3.4	3.4	3.4	5.1	4.8	4.6
Trinidad & Tobago	6.4	6.3	6.2	5.9	5.8	6.1
USA	12.7	13.0	12.5	13.0	13.0	12.1
Other	4.0	4.1	4.0	4.0	4.0	4.0
TOTAL	8.4	8.7	8.5	9.0	9.0	8.8

Source: National Statistical Offices/National Tourist Offices/WTO/OECD/Own Estimates.

Table 75.   **TOTAL POPULATION 1975-1980**

Region 4 : South America

Millions	1975	1976	1977	1978	1979	1980
Argentina	25.38	25.72	26.06	26.39	26.73	27.06
Bolivia	4.89	5.02	5.15	5.29	5.43	5.60
Brazil	106.23	109.18	112.24	115.40	118.65	123.03
Chile	10.20	10.37	10.55	10.73	10.92	11.10
Colombia	23.64	24.33	25.05	25.64	26.36	27.09
Dominican Republic	4.70	4.84	4.98	5.12	5.28	5.43
Ecuador	7.06	7.31	7.56	7.90	8.08	8.35
Guyana	0.78	0.79	0.81	0.82	0.87	0.88
Paraguay	2.65	2.72	2.80	2.89	2.97	3.07
Peru	15.47	15.91	16.36	16.82	17.29	17.78
Suriname	0.36	0.37	0.37	0.37	0.38	0.39
Uruguay	2.82	2.83	2.85	2.86	2.88	2.90
Venezuela	11.99	12.36	12.74	13.12	13.52	13.91
TOTAL	216.17	221.75	227.52	233.35	239.36	246.59

Source: United Nations.

Table 76. TOURIST VISITS
Region 4 : South America

'000	1975	1976	1977	1978	1979	1980
Argentina	1,200	1,303	1,105	1,198	1,019	1,100e
Bolivia	135	158	182	203	210	216e
Brazil	518	556	635	784	1,082	1,120e
Colombia	443	522	709	826	1,151	1,210e
Chile	236	235	297	258	285	269
Ecuador	172	180	202	229	240	243e
El Salvador	285	266	279	293	231	127
Guyana	35	32	32	30	30	32e
Paraguay	93	112	153	182	281	302e
Peru	260	256	265	297	336	413
Suriname	41	55	31	37	48	48e
Uruguay	603	492	690	714	1,104	1,200e
Venezuela	437	535	653	784	820	840e
TOTAL	4,458	4,702	5,233	5,835	6,837	7,120

Source: National Statistical Offices/National Tourist Offices/WTO/OECD/Own Estimates.

Table 77. TOURIST NIGHTS
Region 4 : South America

'000	1975	1976	1977	1978	1979	1980
Argentina	4,536	4,600	4,423	5,071	4,259	4,500e
Bolivia	270	300	341	356	368	380e
Brazil	5,400	5,700	6,000	6,200	8,500	9,000e
Colombia	2,800	2,924	2,689	2,372	2,673	2,700e
Chile	489	566	682	648	640	640e
Ecuador	865	1,156	990	800	740	745e
El Salvador	780	830	850	908	740	400e
Guyana	90	80	80	75	70	72e
Paraguay	225	300	350	365	563	590e
Peru	1,595	1,716	1,613	1,720	1,950	2,300e
Suriname	70	90	50	60	75	75e
Uruguay	650	800	950	1,188	1,600	1,650e
Venezuela	3,800	4,550	5,530	6,630	6,900	7,060e
TOTAL	21,570	23,612	24,548	26,393	29,078	30,112

Source: National Statistical Offices/National Tourist Offices/WTO/OECD/Own Estimates.

Table 78.　　　　　　　**AVERAGE LENGTH OF STAY**

Region 4 : South America

Days	1975	1976	1977	1978	1979	1980
Argentina	3.8	3.5	4.0	4.2	4.2	4.1
Bolivia	2.0	1.9	1.9	1.8	1.8	1.8
Brazil	10.4	10.3	9.4	7.9	7.9	8.0
Colombia	6.3	5.6	3.8	2.9	2.3	2.2
Chile	2.1	2.4	2.3	2.5	2.2	2.4
Ecuador	5.0	6.4	4.9	3.5	3.1	3.1
El Salvador	2.7	3.1	3.0	3.1	3.2	3.1
Guyana	2.6	2.5	2.5	2.5	2.3	2.3
Paraguay	2.4	2.7	2.3	2.0	2.0	2.0
Peru	6.1	6.7	6.1	5.8	5.8	5.6
Suriname	1.7	1.6	1.6	1.6	1.6	1.6
Uruguay	1.1	1.6	1.4	1.7	1.4	1.4
Venezuela	8.7	8.5	8.5	8.5	8.4	8.4
TOTAL	4.8	5.0	4.7	4.5	4.3	4.2

Source: National Statistical Offices/National Tourist Offices/WTO/OECD/Own Estimates.

Table 79.　　　　　　**TOTAL POPULATION 1975-1980**

Region 5 : North Africa & Middle East

Millions	1975	1976	1977	1978	1979	1980
Algeria	16.78	17.30	17.91	17.58	18.19	18.59
Bahrain	0.26	0.27	0.27	0.35	0.29	0.36
Iran	33.38	33.66	34.57	35.50	36.94	37.45
Iraq	11.12	11.51	12.03	12.33	12.77	13.08
Israel	3.46	3.53	3.61	3.69	3.79	3.87
Jordan	2.70	2.78	2.89	2.98	3.09	3.19
Kuwait	1.00	1.06	1.13	1.20	1.27	1.36
Lebanon	2.80	2.87	2.94	3.01	3.09	3.16
Libya	2.43	2.53	2.64	2.74	2.86	2.98
Morocco	17.31	17.83	18.36	18.91	19.47	20.24
Oman	0.77	0.79	0.81	0.84	0.86	0.89
Qatar	0.17	0.18	0.19	0.20	0.21	0.22
Saudi Arabia	7.18	7.40	7.63	7.87	8.11	8.37
Syria	7.44	7.72	8.02	8.33	8.65	8.98
Tunisia	5.61	5.77	5.93	6.08	6.24	6.37
United Arab Emirates	0.56	0.62	0.67	0.71	0.75	0.80
Yemen	5.28	5.40	5.52	5.65	5.79	5.93
Yemen, South	1.71	1.75	1.80	1.85	1.89	1.94
TOTAL	119.96	122.97	126.92	129.82	134.26	137.78

Source: United Nations.

98

Table 80.   TOURIST VISITS

Region 5 : North Africa & Middle East

'000	1975	1976	1977	1978	1979	1980
Algeria	297	185	242	260	175	300
Bahrain	452	466	487	487	500	515e
Iran	560	628	691	618	550	480e
Iraq	482	630	722	720	690	620e
Israel	559	733	894	959	1,009	1,070
Jordan	708	1,063	1,773	1,087	1,203	1,200e
Kuwait	80	88	96	107	114	118e
Lebanon	116	118	122	109	118	115e
Libya	238	145	126	163	175	160e
Morocco	1,245	1,108	1,427	1,477	1,436	1,520
Oman	15	18	20	20	25	26e
Qatar	85	100	115	125	110	116e
Saudi Arabia	895	719	739	750	780	789e
Syria	1,172	1,390	1,249	1,074	1,279	1,150e
Tunisia	1,014	978	1,016	1,142	1,356	1,400
U.A.R.	12	12	15	15	20	22e
Yemen, Rep	25	30	35	38	42	40e
Yemen, Dem	16	18	20	25	28	25e
TOTAL	7,971	8,429	9,789	9,176	9,610	9,666

Source: National Statistical Offices/National Tourist Offices/WTO/OECD/Own Estimates.

Table 81.   **TOURIST NIGHTS**

Region 5 : North Africa & Middle East

'000	1975	1976	1977	1978	1979	1980e
Algeria	1,281	1,384	1,223	1,322	1,297	1,500
Bahrain	1,200	1,250	1,350	1,400	1,435	1,460
Iran	3,921	4,755	4,524	4,500	4,000	3,600
Iraq	1,250	1,250	1,300	1,400	1,200	1,150
Israel	4,160	5,565	6,658	6,887	7,088	7,400
Jordan	5,250	8,000	13,000	8,000	9,000	8,900
Kuwait	300	330	345	366	389	400
Lebanon	406	400	416	412	469	460
Libya	532	299	279	295	310	290
Morocco	4,620	4,116	5,300	5,171	5,456	5,500
Oman	75	85	90	100	125	128
Qatar	500	525	560	582	441	450
Saudi Arabia	1,300	960	1,000	1,050	1,200	1,260
Syria	1,242	1,586	1,341	1,291	1,778	1,620
Tunisia	8,889	8,890	8,118	8,805	11,129	11,600
U.A.R.	60	60	80	80	90	92
Yemen, Rep	145	170	186	210	220	215
Yemen, Dem	51	64	71	90	98	92
TOTAL	35,182	39,689	45,841	41,961	45,725	46,117

Source: National Statistical Offices/National Tourist Offices/WTO/OECD/Own Estimates.

Table 82. **AVERAGE LENGTH OF STAY**

Region 5 : North Africa & Middle East

Days	1975	1976	1977	1978	1979	1980
Algeria	4.3	7.5	5.1	5.1	7.4	5.0
Bahrain	2.7	2.7	2.8	2.9	2.9	2.8
Iran	7.0	7.6	6.5	7.3	7.3	7.5
Iraq	2.6	2.0	1.8	1.9	1.7	1.9
Israel	7.4	7.6	7.4	7.2	7.0	6.9
Jordan	7.4	7.5	7.3	7.4	7.5	7.4
Kuwait	3.8	3.8	3.6	3.4	3.4	3.4
Lebanon	3.5	3.4	3.4	3.8	4.0	4.0
Libya	2.2	2.1	2.2	1.8	1.8	1.8
Morocco	3.7	3.7	3.7	3.5	3.8	3.6
Oman	5.0	4.7	4.5	5.0	5.0	4.9
Qatar	5.9	5.3	4.9	4.7	4.0	3.9
Saudi Arabia	1.5	1.3	1.4	1.4	1.5	1.6
Syria	1.1	1.1	1.1	1.2	1.4	1.4
Tunisia	8.8	9.1	8.0	7.7	8.2	8.3
U.A.R.	5.0	5.0	5.3	5.3	4.5	4.2
Yemen, Rep	5.8	5.7	5.3	5.5	5.2	5.4
Yemen, Dem	3.2	3.6	3.6	3.6	3.5	3.7
TOTAL	4.4	4.7	4.7	4.6	4.8	4.8

Source: National Statistical Offices/National Tourist Offices/WTO/OECD/Own Estimates.

Table 83.　　　　　　　　**TOTAL POPULATION 1975-1980**

Region 6 : Africa

Millions	1975	1976	1977	1978	1979	1980
Angola	6.26	6.41	6.57	6.73	6.90	7.08
Benin	3.11	3.20	3.29	3.38	3.47	3.57
Botswana	0.68	0.71	0.74	0.76	0.79	0.82
Burundi	3.93	4.03	4.14	4.26	4.38	4.51
Cameroon	7.53	7.70	7.91	8.06	8.25	8.50
Central African Republic	1.99	2.03	2.07	2.12	2.17	2.22
Chad	4.03	4.12	4.21	4.31	4.42	4.52
Comoros	0.30	0.31	0.31	0.32	0.33	0.34
Congo	1.35	1.39	1.44	1.46	1.50	1.54
Egypt	37.01	37.87	38.79	39.82	40.98	41.99
Ethiopia	27.47	28.19	28.98	29.71	30.42	31.07
Gambia	0.52	0.54	0.55	0.57	0.58	0.60
Ghana	9.87	10.31	10.63	10.97	11.32	11.45
Ivory Coast	6.71	6.97	7.23	7.61	7.92	7.97
Kenya	13.40	13.85	14.34	14.86	15.32	16.40
Lesotho	1.19	1.21	1.25	1.28	1.31	1.34
Liberia	1.55	1.61	1.66	1.72	1.77	1.87
Madagascar	7.68	7.87	8.08	8.29	8.51	8.74
Malawi	5.24	5.39	5.53	5.67	5.82	5.97
Mali	6.07	6.23	6.39	6.56	6.73	6.91
Mauritius	0.86	0.87	0.88	0.90	0.91	0.96
Mozambique	9.20	9.44	9.68	9.94	10.20	10.47
Namibia	0.88	0.91	0.94	0.97	0.98	1.01
Niger	4.60	4.73	4.86	4.99	5.15	5.31
Nigeria	65.66	67.76	69.94	72.22	74.60	77.08
Senegal	4.98	5.12	5.25	5.38	5.51	5.66
Seychelles	0.06	0.06	0.06	0.06	0.06	0.06
South Africa	25.47	26.13	26.94	27.70	28.48	29.29
Sudan	15.73	16.13	16.95	17.38	17.89	18.69
Swaziland	0.49	0.50	0.51	0.54	0.54	0.55
Tanzania	15.31	16.41	16.92	17.44	17.98	18.40
Togo	2.23	2.29	2.35	2.41	2.47	2.70
Uganda	11.55	11.94	12.35	12.78	13.22	13.20
Upper Volta	6.07	6.23	6.39	6.55	6.73	6.91
Zaire	24.84	25.57	26.31	27.08	27.87	28.29
Zambia	4.98	5.14	5.30	5.47	5.65	5.83
TOTAL	338.80	349.17	359.74	370.27	381.13	391.82

Source: United Nations.

Table 84.			**TOURIST VISITS**			
Region 6 : Africa						

'000	1975	1976	1977	1978	1979	1980e
Angola	180	190	195	200	200	200
Benin	18	19	23	34	41	44
Botswana	110	117	128	147	227	235
Burundi	29	31	39	32	34	35
Cameroon	90	95	101	115	126	128
Central African Rep.	5	5	4	4	5	5
Chad	4	4	5	5	6	6
Comoros	-	-	1	1	1	1
Congo	12	14	15	19	24	24
Egypt	731	913	925	967	1,065	1,220
Ethiopia	20	22	25	29	34	37
Gambia	17	18	20	16	18	20
Ghana	44	56	59	47	53	54
Ivory Coast	109	122	155	179	199	198
Kenya	328	337	346	361	383	390
Lesotho	175	178	180	180	190	195
Liberia	5	6	6	6	6	6
Madagascar	5	5	7	12	11	12
Malawi	58	50	48	47	55	57
Mali	20	20	22	25	28	30
Mauritius	70	75	103	108	123	140
Mozambique	70	72	75	78	80	82
Namibia	48	48	50	55	60	64
Niger	17	18	18	19	19	20
Nigeria	125	114	118	112	120	125
Senegal	155	162	168	194	198	200
Seychelles	35	47	52	62	79	75
S. Africa	578	626	630	680	750	860
Sudan	31	32	35	38	35	36
Swaziland	122	135	118	106	82	88
Tanzania	210	252	260	277	290	320
Togo	57	60	49	59	75	90
Uganda	23	21	20	20	24	24
Upper Volta	15	21	28	36	44	46
Zaire	41	51	52	40	43	46
Zambia	51	56	49	53	55	60
TOTAL	3,608	3,992	4,129	4,363	4,783	5,173

Source: National Statistical Offices/National Tourist Offices/WTO/OECD/Own Estimates.

Table 85.   **TOURIST NIGHTS**

Region 6 : Africa

'000	1975	1976	1977	1978	1979	1980
Angola	250	250	260	260	260	260
Benin	44	43	55	64	78	82
Botswana	200	180	180	190	300	300
Burundi	90	100	120	115	153	158
Cameroon	240	262	230	277	281	289
Central African Rep.	25	25	25	28	30	32
Chad	20	18	20	20	25	25
Comoros	2	3	4	4	7	7
Congo	35	40	44	47	60	62
Egypt	5,409	6,300	6,341	7,137	7,104	8,000
Ethiopia	60	65	75	80	92	96
Gambia	170	180	202	194	210	230
Ghana	400	520	550	420	450	455
Ivory Coast	380	430	550	652	700	690
Kenya	2,240	2,360	2,839	2,913	3,154	3,250
Lesotho	300	300	320	320	335	340
Liberia	50	53	55	59	62	62
Madagascar	28	30	36	45	45	48
Malawi	370	390	385	376	425	440
Mali	51	50	54.	60	68	70
Mauritius	550	600	995	1,052	1,420	1,600
Mozambique	450	480	480	500	520	540
Namibia	150	150	160	160	170	180
Niger	42	44	46	52	50	52
Nigeria	500	450	480	460	475	482
Senegal	606	604	711	886	890	898
Seychelles	316	449	480	485	563	560
S. Africa	1,150	1,250	1,300	1,400	1,550	1,720
Sudan	70	75	80	80	82	82
Swaziland	250	250	270	275	280	290
Tanzania	240	255	295	358	383	392
Togo	148	180	153	212	247	290
Uganda	74	80	80	88	85	88
Upper Volta	80	105	140	190	198	205
Zaire	274	263	205	217	207	215
Zambia	370	372	388	407	415	435
TOTAL	15,634	17,206	18,608	20,083	21,474	22,925

Source: National Statistical Offices/National Tourist Offices/WTO/OECD/Own Estimates.

104

Table 86.

AVERAGE LENGTH OF STAY

Region 6 : Africa

Days	1975	1976	1977	1978	1979	1980
Angola	1.4	1.3	1.3	1.3	1.3	1.3
Benin	2.4	2.3	2.4	1.9	1.9	1.9
Botswana	1.8	1.5	1.4	1.3	1.3	1.3
Burundi	3.1	3.2	3.1	3.6	4.5	4.5
Cameroon	2.7	2.8	2.3	2.4	2.2	2.3
Central African Rep.	5.0	5.0	6.3	7.0	6.0	6.4
Chad	5.0	4.5	4.0	4.0	4.2	4.2
Comoros	2.0	2.0	4.0	4.0	7.0	7.0
Congo	2.9	2.9	2.9	2.5	2.5	2.6
Egypt	7.4	6.9	6.9	7.4	6.7	6.6
Ethiopia	3.0	3.0	3.0	2.8	2.7	2.6
Gambia	10.0	10.0	10.1	12.1	11.7	11.5
Ghana	9.1	9.3	9.3	8.9	8.5	8.4
Ivory Coast	3.5	3.5	3.5	3.6	3.5	3.5
Kenya	6.8	7.0	8.2	8.1	8.2	8.3
Lesotho	1.7	1.7	1.7	1.7	1.7	1.8
Liberia	10.0	8.8	9.2	9.8	10.3	10.3
Madagascar	5.6	6.0	5.1	3.8	4.1	4.0
Malawi	6.4	7.8	8.0	8.0	7.7	7.7
Mali	2.6	2.5	2.5	2.4	2.4	2.3
Mauritius	7.9	8.0	9.7	9.7	11.5	11.4
Mozambique	6.4	6.7	6.4	6.4	6.5	6.6
Namibia	3.1	3.1	3.2	2.9	2.8	2.8
Niger	2.5	2.4	2.6	2.7	2.6	2.6
Nigeria	4.0	3.9	4.1	4.1	4.0	3.9
Senegal	3.9	3.7	4.2	4.6	4.5	4.5
Seychelles	9.0	9.6	9.2	7.8	7.1	7.5
S. Africa	2.0	2.0	2.1	2.1	2.1	2.0
Sudan	2.3	2.3	2.3	2.1	2.3	2.3
Swaziland	2.0	1.9	2.3	2.6	3.4	3.3
Tanzania	1.1	1.0	1.1	1.3	1.3	1.2
Togo	2.6	3.0	3.1	3.6	3.3	3.2
Uganda	3.2	3.8	4.0	4.4	3.5	3.7
Upper Volta	5.3	5.0	5.0	5.3	4.5	4.5
Zaire	6.7	5.2	3.9	5.4	4.8	4.7
Zambia	7.3	6.6	7.9	7.7	7.5	7.3
TOTAL	4.2	4.2	4.4	4.5	4.3	4.2

Source: National Statistical Offices/National Tourist Offices/WTO/OECD/Own Estimates.

Table 87.   **TOTAL POPULATION 1975-1980**

Region 7 : Far East

Millions	1975	1976	1977	1978	1979	1980
Afghanistan	11.78	12.08	12.40	12.72	13.05	13.35
Bangladesh	78.96	80.82	82.72	84.66	86.64	87.66
Bhutan	1.16	1.20	1.23	1.24	1.27	1.30
Brunei	0.16	0.18	0.19	0.20	0.21	0.19
Burma	30.17	30.83	31.51	32.21	32.91	35.30
China	895.34	908.27	920.81	933.03	945.02	956.85
Guam	0.11	0.11	0.11	0.11	0.12	0.12
Hong Kong	4.40	4.44	4.51	4.61	4.90	5.07
India	600.76	613.27	625.82	638.39	650.98	663.60
Indonesia	135.23	138.49	141.78	145.10	148.47	151.89
Japan	111.57	112.77	113.86	114.90	115.87	116.78
Korea, South	35.28	35.86	36.44	37.02	37.60	38.20
Laos	3.30	3.38	3.46	3.55	3.63	3.72
Macau	0.26	0.26	0.26	0.27	0.27	0.28
Malaysia	11.90	12.30	12.60	12.91	13.30	13.44
Maldives	0.13	0.14	0.14	0.15	0.15	0.15
Mongolia	1.44	1.49	1.53	1.57	1.62	1.67
Nepal	12.59	12.86	13.14	13.42	13.71	14.01
Pakistan	70.26	72.37	74.87	76.77	79.84	82.44
Philippines	42.26	43.34	44.42	45.50	46.58	48.40
Samoa	0.15	0.15	0.15	0.15	0.15	0.16
Singapore	2.25	2.28	2.31	2.33	2.36	2.39
Sri Lanka	13.50	13.72	13.94	14.19	14.47	14.74
Taiwan	16.15	16.51	16.81	17.14	17.48	17.62
Thailand	41.87	42.96	44.04	45.10	46.14	47.17
TOTAL	2,120.98	2,160.08	2,199.05	2,237.24	2,276.74	2,316.50

Source: United Nations.

Table 88.   **TOURIST VISITS**

Region 7 : Far East

'000	1975	1976	1977	1978	1979	1980
Afghanistan	91	91	117	92	37	42e
Bangladesh	64	37	45	50	57	62e
Bhutan	2	2	2	3	3	3e
Brunei	3	3	3	4	5	6e
Burma	17	18	20	20	22	23e
China	20	40	75	120	160	200
Guam	228	201	240	233	264	273e
Hong Kong	1,301	1,560	1,756	2,055	2,213	2,301
India	465	534	640	748	765	800e
Indonesia	366	401	433	469	501	657
Japan	708	795	1,028	1,094	1,113	1,317
Korea, S	633	834	950	1,079	979	980e
Laos	15	16	16	15	15	15e
Macau	300	350	360	564	644	680e
Malaysia	1,183	1,225	1,289	1,399	1,416	1,530
Maldives	22	25	27	29	35	38e
Mongolia	145	150	160	150	155	160e
Nepal	90	92	129	156	162	168
Pakistan	172	197	220	291	319	335e
Philippines	502	615	711	840	900	1,122
Samoa	11	10	25	24	23	23e
Singapore	1,029	1,162	1,682	2,047	2,247	2,500
Sri Lanka	103	119	154	193	250	330
Taiwan	717	854	934	1,046	1,097	1,120e
Thailand	1,178	1,098	1,221	1,452	1,591	1,900
TOTAL	9,365	10,429	12,237	14,173	14,973	16,585

Source: National Statistical Offices/National Tourist Offices/WTO/OECD/Own Estimates.

Table 89.

TOURIST NIGHTS

Region 7 : Far East

'000	1975	1976	1977	1978	1979	1980(e)
Afghanistan	819	1,183	1,520	1,200	410	425
Bangladesh	54	60	63	68	72	75
Bhutan	10	10	10	12	12	12
Brunei	15	15	16	18	20	22
Burma	60	60	80	80	85	86
China	100	200	300	500	650	820
Guam	1,254	1,105	1,320	1,271	1,505	1,600
Hong Kong	4,814	6,084	6,850	8,000	8,600	8,900
India	12,555	14,420	16,250	18,850	19,584	20,250
Indonesia	2,300	2,600	2,800	3,000	3,500	4,500
Japan	3,341	3,750	3,887	3,627	3,698	3,950
Korea, S	1,780	2,340	2,702	2,928	3,101	3,200
Laos	60	60	60	60	60	60
Macau	280	340	349	598	793	810
Malaysia	2,172	1,646	2,200	2,500	2,600	2,750
Maldives	150	160	180	190	210	225
Mongolia	450	460	460	450	450	455
Nepal	264	309	325	406	455	462
Pakistan	170	240	259	343	374	395
Philippines	3,114	3,100	3,600	4,490	4,800	5,700
Samoa	50	50	75	75	75	75
Singapore	2,300	2,550	3,800	4,650	5,000	5,500
Sri Lanka	731	926	1,109	1,469	1,787	2,400
Taiwan	5,000	6,000	6,500	7,300	7,639	7,900
Thailand	5,300	5,000	5,520	6,793	8,098	9,250
TOTAL	47,143	52,668	60,235	68,878	73,578	79,822

Source: National Statistical Offices/National Tourist Offices/WTO/OECD/Own Estimates.

Table 90.   AVERAGE LENGTH OF STAY

Region 7 : Far East

Days	1975	1976	1977	1978	1979	1980
Afghanistan	9.0	13.0	13.0	13.0	11.1	10.1
Bangladesh	0.8	1.6	1.4	1.4	1.3	1.2
Bhutan	5.0	5.0	5.0	4.0	4.0	4.0
Brunei	5.0	5.0	5.3	4.5	4.0	3.7
Burma	3.5	3.3	4.0	4.0	3.9	3.7
China	5.0	5.0	4.0	4.2	4.1	4.1
Guam	5.5	5.5	5.5	5.7	5.7	5.9
Hong Kong	3.7	3.9	3.9	3.9	3.9	3.9
India	27.0	27.0	25.4	25.2	25.6	25.3
Indonesia	6.3	6.5	6.5	6.4	7.0	6.8
Japan	4.7	4.7	3.8	3.3	3.3	3.0
Korea (S)	2.8	2.8	2.8	2.7	3.2	3.3
Laos	4.0	3.8	3.8	4.0	4.0	4.0
Macau	0.9	1.0	1.0	1.1	1.2	1.2
Malaysia	1.8	1.3	1.7	1.8	1.8	1.8
Maldives	6.8	6.4	6.7	6.6	6.0	5.9
Mongolia	3.1	3.1	2.9	3.0	2.9	2.8
Nepal	2.9	3.4	2.5	2.6	2.8	2.8
Pakistan	1.0	1.2	1.2	1.2	1.2	1.2
Philippines	6.2	5.0	5.1	5.3	5.3	5.1
Samoa	4.5	5.0	3.0	3.1	3.3	3.3
Singapore	2.2	2.2	2.3	2.3	2.2	2.2
Sri Lanka	7.1	7.8	7.2	7.6	7.1	7.3
Taiwan	7.0	7.0	7.0	7.0	7.0	7.1
Thailand	4.5	4.6	4.5	4.7	5.1	4.9
TOTAL	5.0	5.1	4.9	4.9	4.9	4.8

Source: National Statistical Offices/National Tourist Offices/WTO/OECD/Own Estimates.

Table 91. **TOTAL POPULATION 1975-1980**

Region 8 : Oceania

Millions	1975	1976	1977	1978	1979	1980
Australia	13.77	13.92	14.07	14.25	14.42	14.62
Cook Islands	0.02	0.02	0.02	0.02	0.02	0.02
Fiji	0.57	0.59	0.60	0.61	0.62	0.63
French Polynesia	0.13	0.14	0.14	0.15	0.15	0.16
Hawaii	0.89	0.89	0.90	0.90	0.90	0.90
New Caledonia	0.13	0.13	0.14	0.14	0.14	0.15
New Zealand	3.07	3.09	3.11	3.11	3.10	3.10
Papua New Guinea	2.76	2.83	2.91	2.99	3.08	3.08
Solomon Islands	0.19	0.20	0.21	0.21	0.22	0.22
Tonga	0.10	0.09	0.09	0.09	0.10	0.10
Vanuatu	0.10	0.10	0.10	0.10	0.10	0.11
Western Samoa	0.15	0.15	0.15	0.15	0.16	0.16
TOTAL	21.88	22.15	22.44	22.72	23.01	23.25

Source: United Nations.

Table 92.   TOURIST VISITS

Region 8 : Oceania

'000	1975	1976	1977	1978	1979	1980
Australia	516	532	563	631	793	903
Cook Islands	8	10	15	17	18	20e
Fiji	107	107	109	184	189	194e
French Polynesia	83	92	91	94	101	105e
Hawaii	2,829	3,220	3,435	3,670	3,961	4,320e
New Caledonia	32	35	40	47	55	59e
New Hebrides	15	18	25	35	40	44e
New Zealand	360	373	388	404	427	460e
Papua New Guinea	20	26	30	34	33	39
Solomon Islands	6	7	7	8	10	12e
Tonga	10	10	11	12	12	12e
Western Samoa	19	23	22	25	28	30e
TOTAL	4,005	4,453	4,736	5,161	5,667	6,198

Source: National Statistical Offices/National Tourist Offices/WTO/OECD/Own Estimates.

Table 93.   TOURIST NIGHTS

Region 8 : Oceania

'000	1975	1976	1977	1978	1979	1980
Australia	22,350	25,000	21,700	24,000	28,000	32,600e
Cook Islands	55	70	110	125	135	145e
Fiji	900	920	940	1,656	1,700	1,800e
French Polynesia	528	596	662	685	787	860e
Hawaii	23,035	26,852	31,678	35,041	40,800	44,500e
New Caledonia	325	360	400	482	489	500e
New Hebrides	110	135	185	260	300	325e
New Zealand	5,800	6,050	6,300	6,500	6,800	7,250e
Papua New Guinea	160	220	250	290	320	370e
Solomon Islands	35	42	45	50	60	68e
Tonga	80	80	90	96	95	96e
Western Samoa	112	144	135	160	180	195e
TOTAL	53,490	60,469	62,495	69,345	79,666	88,709

Source: National Statistical Offices/National Tourist Offices/WTO/OECD/Own Estimates.

Table 94.　　　　　　　　AVERAGE LENGTH OF STAY

Region 8 : Oceania

Days	1975	1976	1977	1978	1979	1980
Australia	43.3	47.0	38.5	38.0	35.3	36.1
Cook Islands	6.9	7.0	7.3	7.4	7.5	7.3
Fiji	8.4	8.6	8.6	9.0	9.0	9.3
French Polynesia	6.4	6.5	7.3	7.3	7.8	8.2
Hawaii	8.1	8.3	9.2	9.5	10.3	10.3
New Caledonia	10.2	10.3	10.0	10.3	8.9	8.5
New Hebrides	7.3	7.5	7.4	7.4	7.5	7.4
New Zealand	16.1	16.2	16.2	16.1	15.9	15.8
Papua New Guinea	8.0	8.5	8.3	8.5	9.7	9.5
Solomon Islands	5.8	6.0	6.4	6.3	6.0	5.7
Tonga	8.0	8.0	8.2	8.0	7.9	8.0
Western Samoa	5.9	6.3	6.1	6.4	6.4	6.5
TOTAL	13.4	13.6	13.2	13.4	14.1	14.3

Source: National Statistical Offices/National Tourist Offices/WTO/OECD/Own Estimates.

CHAPTER FIVE
METHODS OF TRAVEL

The boom in world travel demand has been strongly interlinked with the growth and development of the world air transport industry, which depends for its livelihood on the international movement of tourist travel. In this chapter, therefore, I shall be looking at the size and structure of the airline industry, which having faced unprecedented growth in the 1970's, is now severely hit by competition and recession. I shall also be looking briefly at the car rental industry, which is itself heavily dependent on air travel and currently facing similar problems.

Before looking in more detail at air travel, I want to begin by considering what proportion of the total tourist arrivals to each country use air transport as their method of arrival, and look at some specific national examples. Figures on this subject are not comprehensive but a fair number of countries do publish information on method of arrival, whether air, road, rail or sea.

The main considerations here appear to be geographical. Obviously if a country is landlocked, it is unlikely to witness the arrival of many visitors by sea. If a country is thousands of miles from its principal sources of visitors, most arrivals are likely to be by air. Islands, generally, receive most visitors by air because sea travel is an impractical alternative for holiday travellers unless a cruise is involved. The extent of air travel is also dependent on whether the country is a primary or secondary choice of destination; countries which are frequently visited by tourists from neighbouring countries which are perhaps more popular tourist destinations are likely to display more land arrivals. And the presence within the country of a major international airport or airline will be an important factor, too.

If we exclude the smaller islands such as Cyprus and Iceland, a low proportion of arrivals to the countries of **Western Europe** are by air. In the Mediterranean, most arrivals are by road, with only Greece showing a sizeable percentage of air transport arrivals. Air transport to Scandinavia is also high, accounting for three-quarters of arrivals to Norway, and over half to Finland.

60% of tourist arrivals to the United Kingdom are by air, which is less than one would expect for an island because of the country's proximity to the European continent. Five year figures for the United Kingdom show the steadily increasing importance of air travel to the country.

Few arrivals to countries in **Eastern Europe** are by air, only about 7-8% overall. Most tourists arrive by land, mainly by road. Over 90% of arrivals to Yugoslavia, which is the most obvious holiday attraction, are by land. This is because most tourists visiting countries in the Eastern bloc come from other countries either in Eastern Europe or on the European continent.

Table 95. Arrivals to the United Kingdom by Method of Transport

	Air	Sea	Total
	'000	'000	'000
1976			
1977	7,229	5,052	12,281
1978	7,580	5,067	12,646
1979	7,614	4,872	12,486
1980			

Source: International Passenger Survey, Department of Trade & Industry, London

As an example of travel away from West Europe, France seems to offer a good balance, a major travelling population possessing good air, rail and road transport facilities. Travel overseas by the French is, in fact, heavily concentrated on air transport, even for travel within the European continent. Around 75% of travel by the French to countries in Western Europe is by air, and this rises to over 90% for travel outside Europe.

Table 96. Travel to Other Countries by the French — Method of Transport in 1978

	Air	Train	Sea	Road	Other	Total
West Europe	72.9	5.4	4.6	7.5	9.5	100.0
Eastern Europe	93.3	0.1	0.4	1.6	4.6	100.0
Middle East	80.3	-	17.3	-	2.4	100.0
North Africa	94.0	-	3.1	0.3	2.5	100.0
North America	91.7	-	4.5	-	3.8	100.0
South America	97.9	-	0.4	-	1.7	100.0
Oceania	93.5	-	-	-	6.5	100.0
Africa	94.3	-	1.8	-	3.9	100.0
Asia	100.0	-	-	-	-	100.0

Source: "Statistiques du Commerce" INSEE, Paris

The situation is very different in **North and Central America**. Here, a large number of tourist arrivals are by air, particularly to the Caribbean; virtually all arrivals in Jamaica, Haiti, Antigua, Aruba and Barbados are by air.

But air transport is less significant within the countries of the North American sub-continent, where land arrivals are again important because of inter-country travel between the U.S.A., Canada and Mexico. Destinations are very important, and this is demonstrated by an evaluation of the transport methods used by Canadian tourists returning to Canada in 1974 from, firstly, the U.S.A., and secondly, from other countries. We can see that whilst land transport accounts for 80% of returns from the U.S.A., virtually all returns from other countries are by air.

Table 97. Canadian Tourist Returning to Canada: Method of Transport 1974

		'000s	%
From the USA	— by car	6,275	59.4
	— by bus	565	5.3
	— by rail	36	0.3
	— by other land means	470	4.4
	— Total Land	7,346	69.5
	— by air	1,579	14.9
	— by sea	209	2.0
Total U.S.A.		9,134	86.4
From other countries	— by land	25	0.2
	— by air	1,390	13.2
	— by sea	19	0.2
Total Other Countries		1,434	13.6
Grand Total		10,568	100.0

Source: "Travel Between Canada and Other Countries", Statistics Canada
Note that excursionists have been excluded

Travel by Americans overseas — or at least to other countries — is about 50% by air, and 45% by land, according to the 1977 National Travel Survey.

Table 98. Household Trips Outside the United States 1977: Method of Transport

	'000 Household Trips	% of Total
Auto	3,447	33.3
Truck	568	5.5
Bus	466	4.5
Train	72	0.7
Airplane	5,334	51.5
Other	475	4.6
Total	10,364	100.0

Source: National Travel Survey, U.S. Bureau of the Census

Figures on arrivals into **South America** present a fairly mixed bag; air transport accounts for 85% of Peruvian arrivals, but under 30% of arrivals to Colombia and Uruguay, where land arrivals are again important. The high percentage for Peru is undoubtedly due to its popularity as a holiday destination among Europeans and the same pattern is demonstrated in Suriname, which receives two-thirds of its tourist visits from Western Europe, and over 80% of its arrivals by air.

Similar contracts exist in **North Africa and the Middle East**, with the share of visitors arriving by air varying considerably. The proportion of air travellers was, however, more consistently high in the **Far East**, particularly to Taiwan, Sri Lanka, Singapore, South Korea and India. These countries have good airline systems and many visitors from The Americas and Europe. Finally, **Oceania** also shows an expectedly high incidence of air arrivals, accounting for virtually all arrivals to the Pacific Islands, and Australasia. This is as one would expect when the only alternative is sea transport, and the distances considerable.

The importance of distance is emphasised when we look at figures on Australians returning to Australia from other countries in 1978. With a straight choice between air and sea, most inevitably choose air, and the proportion returning by air is 98.8%. But it is interesting to observe that 10% of returns from Singapore are by sea, as returning tourists take advance of cheaper fares through the Far East.

116

Table 99. Short Stay Movement of Australian Residents Returning from Overseas Countries: Method of Transport in 1978

	By Sea	By Air	Total
Africa	11	8,990	9,001
The Americas	470	123,056	123,526
Asia — Total	6,130	210,283	216,413
— Hong Kong	525	41,703	42,228
— Japan	676	14,780	15,455
— Singapore	4,272	36,825	41,097
Europe — Total	3,318	327,084	330,402
— UK / Eire	2,995	186,813	189,808
Oceania — Total	1,596	336,982	338,578
— New Zealand	775	205,570	206,345
Total	12,212	1,017,270	1,029,482

Source: Australian Bureau of Statistics 1978

Before going on to look in more detail at world air travel, I have included here some figures on international fare payments. These cover the amounts spent by overseas visitors in the country concerned (i.e. credits) and the amounts spent on travel services by the residents of the country in other countries (debits).

Most countries in **Western Europe** have a positive balance in terms of passenger fare payments and receipts. The Mediterranean countries showed a good credit balance, but the United Kingdom was well ahead with a fare balance of over 1,000 million dollars in 1980.

Figures were not available for **Eastern Europe**, and only a few were available for **North and Central America**. Here, both the U.S.A. and Mexico spend considerably more in fare payments overseas than they recover from visitors.

Fairly complete figures for **South America** show that most countries had a deficit in terms of international fare payments, most notable Argentina and Brazil. Even Peru has a deficit of 13 million dollars despite being a popular tourist destination.

Table 100. METHOD OF ARRIVAL 1979/80

Western Europe

	Air	Road	Rail	Sea	Total
Austria	1%	93%	6%	-	100%
Cyprus	94%	-	-	6%	100%
Finland	52%	17%	-	31%	100%
Gibraltar	42%	-	-	58%	100%
Greece	61%	18%	2%	19%	100%
Iceland	100%	-	-	-	100%
Ireland	58%	1%	-	41%	100%
Italy	10%	75%	14%	1%	100%
Malta	96%	-	-	4%	100%
Norway	76%	-	-	24%	100%
Portugal	20%	73%	1%	6%	100%
San Marino	-	100%	-	-	100%
Spain	25%	66%	6%	3%	100%
Turkey	30%	34%	5%	31%	100%
UK	61%	-	-	39%	100%

Source: WTO/OECD/National Offices.

Table 101. METHOD OF ARRIVAL 1979/80

Eastern Europe

	Air	Road	Rail	Sea	Total
Bulgaria	12%	68%	19%	1%	100%
Czechoslovakia	2%	78%	20%	-	100%
Hungary	3%	72%	25%	-	100%
Poland	4%	75%	19%	2%	100%
Rumania	10%	55%	31%	4%	100%
Yugoslavia	4%	87%	6%	3%	100%

Source: WTO/OECD/National Offices.

Table 102.   **METHOD OF ARRIVAL 1979/1980**

North & Central America

	Air	Road	Rail	Sea	Total
Antigua	98%	-	-	2%	100%
Aruba	99%	-	-	1%	100%
Barbados	98%	-	-	2%	100%
Bermuda	77%	-	-	23%	100%
British Virgin Islands	51%	-	-	49%	100%
Canada	24%	73%	1%	2%	100%
Costa Rica	45%	——54%——		1%	100%
Dominica	96%	-	-	4%	100%
Grenada	93%	-	-	7%	100%
Guatemala	44%	56%	-	-	100%
Haiti	100%	-	-	-	100%
Jamaica	100%	-	-	-	100%
Martinique	68%	-	-	32%	100%
Mexico	60%	40%	-	-	100%
Panama	82%	18%	-	-	100%
Puerto Rico	77%	-	-	23%	100%
St. Kitts	89%	-	-	11%	100%
Trinidad & Tobago	100%	-	-	-	100%
U.S.A.	50%	——48%——		2%	100%

Source: WTO/OECD/National Offices

Table 103.   **METHOD OF ARRIVAL 1979/1980**

South America

	Air	Road	Rail	Sea	Total
Argentina	70%	—— 6%——		24%	100%
Bolivia	48%	——52%——		-	100%
Brazil	58%	——40%——		2%	100%
Colombia	28%	72%	-	-	100%
Chile	41%	53%	5%	1%	100%
Dom. Republic	64%	-	-	36%	100%
Ecuador	64%	35%	-	1%	100%
El Salvador	27%	71%	-	2%	100%
Paraguay	26%	72%	-	2%	100%
Peru	85%	13%	-	2%	100%
Suriname	82%	18%	-	-	100%
Uruguay	29%	41%	-	30%	100%

Source: WTO/OECD/National Offices

Table 104.   **METHOD OF ARRIVAL 1979/1980**

North Africa & Middle East

	Air	Road	Rail	Sea	Total
Algeria	70%	22%	-	8%	100%
Bahrain	90%	-	-	10%	100%
Iran	63%	34%	-	2%	100%
Israel	86%	1%	-	13%	100%
Jordan	26%	70%	1%	3%	100%
Kuwait	26%	72%	-	2%	100%
Morocco	44%	33%	-	23%	100%
Syria	9%	88%	-	3%	100%
Tunisia	79%	15%	-	6%	100%

Source: WTO/OECD/National Offices

Table 105.   **METHOD OF ARRIVAL 1979/1980**
Africa

	Air	Road	Rail	Sea	Total
Benin	24%	74%	1%	1%	100%
Botswana	20%	71%	9%	-	100%
Burundi	39%	——53%——		8%	100%
Cameroon	76%	17%	-	7%	100%
Egypt	81%	4%	-	15%	100%
Ethiopia	100%	-	-	-	100%
Gambia	68%	23%	-	9%	100%
Ghana	84%	16%	-	-	100%
Ivory Coast	100%	-	-	-	100%
Kenya	90%	8%	-	2%	100%
Madagascar	100%	-	-	-	100%
Malawi	53%	46%	1%	-	100%
Mauritius	100%	-	-	-	100%
Seychelles	100%	-	-	-	100%
Togo	77%	23%	-	-	100%
Zaire	73%	27%	-	-	100%
Zambia	45%	53%	1%	1%	100%

Source: WTO/OECD/National Offices

Table 106. METHOD OF ARRIVAL 1979/1980

Far East

	Air	Road	Rail	Sea	Total
Afghanistan	26%	74%	-	-	100%
Bangladesh	60%	40%	-	-	100%
Guam	97%	-	-	3%	100%
Hong Kong	93%	——5%——		2%	100%
India	88%	5%	1%	6%	100%
Indonesia	95%	-	-	5%	100%
Korea, S.	98%	-	-	2%	100%
Macau	-	12%	-	88%	100%
Malaysia	38%	36%	20%	6%	100%
Nepal	85%	15%	-	-	100%
Pakistan	57%	23%	20%	-	100%
Philippines	98%	-	-	2%	100%
Singapore	83%	11%	-	6%	100%
Sri Lanka	90%	-	-	10%	100%
Taiwan	99%	-	-	1%	100%
Thailand	81%	8%	-	1%	100%

Source: WTO/OECD/National Offices

Table 107. METHOD OF ARRIVAL 1979/1980

Oceania

	Air	Road	Rail	Sea	Total
Australia	98%	-	-	2%	100%
Cayman Islands	63%	-	-	37%	100%
Cook Islands	100%	-	-	-	100%
French Polynesia	99%	-	-	1%	100%
Hawaii	100%	-	-	-	100%
New Caledonia	100%	-	-	-	100%
New Zealand	99%	-	-	1%	100%
Papua New Guinea	99%	-	-	1%	100%
Tonga	25%	-	-	75%	100%

Source: WTO/OECD/National Offices.

Table 108.   Balance of Payments: Passenger Fare Payments in Western Europe 1980

(million dollars)	Credits Less Debits
Belgium	- 73
Cyprus	+ 32
Finland	+ 52
West Germany	- 208
Greece	+ 69
Iceland	+ 70
Italy	+ 705
Malta	+ 43
Netherlands	+ 135
Portugal	+ 69
Spain	+ 254
Sweden	- 2
Turkey	- 3
United Kingdom	+ 1,035

Table 109.   Balance of Payments: Passenger Fares in North and Central America 1980

(million dollars)	Credits Less Debits
Bahamas	+ 15
Barbados	-
Costa Rica	- 7
Guatemala	- 36
Jamaica	+ 47
Mexico	- 138
Trinidad & Tobago	+ 24
USA	- 1,041

Source: IMF

Table 110. Balance of Payments: Passenger Fares in South America

(million dollars)	Credits Less Debits
Argentina	- 260
Bolivia	+ 5
Brazil	- 180
Colombia	+ 43
Chile	+ 11
Ecuador	- 13
El Salvador	0
Peru	- 13
Suriname	- 2
Uruguay	- 33
Venezuela	- 67

Out of the figures available for Africa and the Middle East, few countries show a surplus in terms of passenger fare payments. The exceptions are Kuwait, with a considerable credit balance of 108 million dollars.

Out of the available figures for Africa and the Middle East, countries in the latter area showed better balances than in Africa.

Several countries in **North Africa and Middle East** showed healthy balances on their international fare payments, notably Kuwait, Israel, Tunisia and Jordan. **Africa** revealed generally poor results for the countries surveyed.

A few figures only are available for **Far East** and **Oceania**. They show debits for main travelling nations like Japan and New Zealand, with South Korea coming out best with a surplus balance of over 300 million dollars.

Table 111. Balance of Payments: Passenger Fare Payments in North Africa and Middle East in 1980

(million dollars)	Credits Less Debits
Israel	+ 67
Jordan	+ 86
Kuwait	+ 108
Libya	- 79
Morocco	+ 17
Tunisia	+ 72
Yemen	+ 4
. . . . . and in Africa	
Botswana	- 2
Congo	- 11
Ghana	- 7
Kenya	+ 23
Madagascar	- 22
Mauritius	- 4
South Africa	+ 15
Zambia	- 54

Table 112. Balance of Payments: Passenger Fares in Far East and Oceania

(million dollars)	Credits Less Debits
Japan	- 963
Korea, South	+ 305
Malaysia	+ 5
Nepal	+ 2
Philippines	- 96
Sri Lanka	- 10
Thailand	- 17
Fiji	+ 6
New Zealand	- 36

Table 113.   PASSENGER SERVICES CREDIT

Western Europe

$m	1975	1976	1977	1978	1979	1980
Belgium*	130	134	162	229	306	422
Cyprus	7	17	22	31	44	63
Denmark	39	42	37	48		
Finland	56	76	100	124	174	194
W. Germany	886	993	1,168	1,327	1,615	1,926
Greece	51	35	42	61	45	72
Iceland	65	69	85	101	110	70
Ireland	75	83	93	125	154	
Italy	521	514	646	727	893	1,050
Malta	10	10	14	23	33	43
Netherlands	452	514	565	627	722	924
Norway	256	298	337	418	594	709
Portugal	28	25	36	44	39	79
Spain	300	327	361	438	518	480
Sweden	282	305	328	421	451	381
Turkey	85	89	44	50	96	36
UK	1,230	1,353	1,486	1,948	2,353	2,917

Source: IMF.

Table 114. PASSENGER SERVICES DEBIT
Western Europe

$m	1975	1976	1977	1978	1979	1980
Belgium*	119	122	177	245	292	495
Cyprus	13	16	20	23	27	31
Finland	50	61	79	91	115	142
W. Germany	959	1,108	1,296	1,578	1,873	2,134
Greece	24	8	4	3	6	3
Italy	132	167	188	235	295	345
Malta	5	5	6	9	9	10
Netherlands	353	411	465	543	633	789
Portugal	24	18	16	16	12	10
Spain	85	96	89	139	202	226
Sweden	169	160	203	263	332	383
Turkey	29	30	28	15	17	39
UK	744	670	776	947	1,402	1,882

Source: IMF

Table 115. PASSENGER SERVICES CREDIT
North & Central America

$m	1975	1976	1977	1978	1979	1980
Bahamas	3	3	3	4	5	7
Barbados	4	4	4	8	11	13
Costa Rica	6	7	8	9	10	10
Guatemala	-	-	17	19	24	25
Honduras	1	4	5	6	8	8
Jamaica	36	36	28	55	67	62
Mexico	90	90	106	131	159	223
Nicaragua	2	5	4	4	4	
Panama	14	15	16	18	19	
Trinidad & Tobago	31	35	41	25	45	
USA	1,032	1,235	1,378	1,590	2,145	2,564

Source: IMF.

Table 116. PASSENGER SERVICES DEBIT
North & Central America

$m	1975	1976	1977	1978	1979	1980
Bahamas	5	12	14	22	28	22
Barbados	7	7	6	9	11	13
Costa Rica	9	12	14	15	16	17
Guatemala	21	23	31	33	50	61
Haiti	4	6	8	15	18	29
Honduras	1	2	2	3	3	4
Jamaica	15	20	18	11	14	15
Mexico	135	143	126	184	244	361
Nicaragua	6	6	7	8	6	
Panama	15	17	18	20	20	
Trinidad & Tobago	12	12	12	20	21	
USA	2,271	2,563	2,744	2,905	3,191	3,605

Source: IMF.

Table 117. PASSENGER SERVICES CREDIT
South America

$m	1975	1976	1977	1978	1979	1980
Argentina	40	44	107	94	79	115
Bolivia	3	4	7	9	19	21
Brazil	30	16	28	43	57	57
Colombia	49	50	55	76	84	77
Chile	1	1	4	30	35	42
Ecuador	7	7	12	15	18	21
El Salvador	6	6	5	7	11	
Peru	16	16	20	24	28	
Suriname	1	1	1	1	2	28
Uruguay				3	3	
Venezuela		16	32	33	49	66

Source: IMF.

Table 118.   PASSENGER SERVICES DEBIT

South America

$m	1975	1976	1977	1978	1979	1980
Argentina	161	73	121	148	278	377
Bolivia	6	6	9	10	13	16
Brazil	98	111	128	128	156	237
Colombia	22	24	35	36	48	34
Chile	15	22	36	43	49	66
Ecuador	15	18	18	22	29	34
El Salvador	13	9	10	10	11	
Paraguay	4	5	7	8	13	17
Peru	56	43	54	39	41	
Suriname	19	8	9	10	13	30
Uruguay	14	14	15	20	35	
Venezuela		72	67	105	111	133

Source: IMF

Table 119.   PASSENGER SERVICES CREDIT

North Africa &Middle East

$m	1975	1976	1977	1978	1979	1980
Iran	174	193	250			
Israel	107	148	179	165	195	202
Jordan	35	48	57	87	129	192
Kuwait	52	72	74	84	94	144
Libya			16	19	18	
Morocco	29	25	41	49	61	85
Saudi Arabia				382	589	737
Tunisia		70	72	96	125	133
Yemen, Republic	2	2	2	10	12	7
Yemen, Dem					14	

Source: IMF

Table 120.   PASSENGER SERVICES DEBIT

North Africa &Middle East

$m	1975	1976	1977	1978	1979	1980
Iran		490	528			
Israel	30	51	57	75	109	135
Jordan	33	34	40	60	76	106
Kuwait	21	24	28	33	36	36
Libya	45	44	104	99	97	
Morocco	30	31	37	44	61	68
Tunisia		46	56	58	66	61
Yemen, Republic	1	1	1	1	1	3
Yemen, Dem	2	2	2	2	3	

Source: IMF

Table 121.   PASSENGER SERVICES CREDIT

Africa

$m	1975	1976	1977	1978	1979	1980
Botswana	2	2	6	5	4	4
Central African Republic			1			
Congo					5	7
Ethiopia	22	28	31	32	36	49
Ghana					7	
Kenya	60	48	26	59	47	83
Madagascar	8	10	1		1	
Malawi	10	3				
Mali	4	4	7	9	11	
Mauritius			1	9	10	9
S. Africa	84	94	110	136	181	217
Swaziland					1	
Upper Volta				1		
Zambia	12	16	16	15	26	21

Source: IMF

Table 122. PASSENGER SERVICES DEBIT

Africa

$m	1975	1976	1977	1978	1979	1980
Benin	3	3	3			
Botswana	4	1	2	2	7	6
Central African Republic	8	8	10	11	10	17
Chad	8	6	6			
Congo	17	17	14	14	18	18
Gambia	1	1	2	2	1	
Ghana					14	
Ivory Coast	47	42	58	70	92	
Kenya	32	38	21	45	41	60
Madagascar	18	20	16	18	23	
Malawi	9	8				
Mali	4	4				
Mauritius	10	11	12	13	14	13
Niger	6	7				
Senegal	28	29	32			
Seychelles		1	1	2	3	3
S. Africa	138	102	124	119	160	202
Swaziland				1	1	1
Togo	5	6				
Uganda	12	3	5	6	12	6
Upper Volta	12	12	14	22		
Zambia	41	48	49	53	81	75

Source: IMF

Table 123. PASSENGER SERVICES CREDIT

Far East

$m	1975	1976	1977	1978	1979	1980
Burma	2	1	3	3	2	
Japan	231	300	350	413	517	521
Korea (S)	76	72	107	116	240	351
Malaysia	42	53	65	83	75	120
Nepal		3	3	5	7	9
Philippines Samoa	8	7	5	6	8	13
Sri Lanka	4	4	4	1	1	2
Thailand	29	18	13	14	49	49

Source: IMF

Table 124. PASSENGER SERVICES DEBIT

Far East

$m	1975	1976	1977	1978	1979	1980
Japan	631	774	852	1,039	1,512	1,484
Korea (S)	13	16	33	59	57	46
Malaysia	44	42	46	69	102	115
Nepal		3	3	5	7	7
Philippines Samoa			44	60	123	109
Sri Lanka	3	3	3	8	10	12
Thailand	18	14	23	36	48	66

Source: IMF

Table 125.   PASSENGER SERVICES CREDIT

Oceania

$m	1975	1976	1977	1978	1979	1980
Fiji	8	9	9	13	15	17
New Zealand	87	109	119	135	142	177
Papua New Guinea		5	7	7	7	7

Source: IMF.

Table 126.   PASSENGER SERVICES DEBIT

Oceania

$m	1975	1976	1977	1978	1979	1980
Fiji	10	9	9	10	10	11
New Zealand	106	111	127	140	172	213
Papua New Guinea		13	16	15	15	18

Source: IMF.

I want now to consider in more detail the movement of air traffic around the world. Firstly, a note about definition. The figures presented here refer to all passengers carried, on international routes, by main routes, by country, and by main airline. This would, of course, include all tourists who travel by air, but it would also include the looser categories of visitors to other countries which are outside the scope of this book. Such types of visitors would include people travelling to a country for a lengthy stay of a year or more, such as students or businessmen. It would also include, of course, emigrants. Generally speaking, however, these would form only a small proportion of total air traffic and this does not detract from the value of the following analyses.

Two international bodies collect and publish statistics on world air travel. Firstly, there is the International Air Transport Association (IATA) whose 110 members include all the major world airlines. The statistics they cover mainly concentrate on their members, but they offer the best guide to route movements and the performance of IATA members is generally considered to be a more than adequate barometer of progress within the industry as a whole.

The second main source is the International Civil Aviation Organisation (ICAO) which is the air travel organisation of the United Nations. They publish statistics for all airlines, but have less detailed information on routes and types of seats available.

AIR TRANSPORT

The world demand for air transport mounted rapidly in the late 60's and 1970's as levels of world tourism increased. The growth in world tourist traffic especially suited the airlines because as the travel industry expanded, so did the demand for longer and more adventurous holidays, in countries further afield. And at the same time, the growing internationalism of world trade ensured an expanding and prosperous business sector. The major world airlines were able to maximise the potential demand with a range of services which catered for everyone from the exclusive business traveller to the inclusive holidaymaker.

The problems which the airline industry encountered in 1980 were in some ways inevitable and in others unfortunate. The problem with any growth industry is that it attracts more suppliers, so an increase in demand becomes an essential element in market progress if all the concerns within the market are to continue to progress well. Should there be a levelling off in demand, as has occurred in demand for air travel, then the market will become more competitive and all concerns will suffer until some of them are forced to give way.

Such problems have been compounded in the air travel industry, not so much by the severity of the decline in demand (in fact, there has been no decline) but by various factors beyond the control of the industry itself. The most important of these has been the energy crisis, which from 1973 onwards substantially raised operating costs. The rise in fuel costs could not simply be passed on to the consumer because this would have involved sharp increases in ticket prices which would have resulted in a fall in demand. Also, unlike the petroleum industry, the airline industry was not providing an essential commodity, and could not justify price increases on investment grounds, being merely an end-user. But price increases might well have been the inevitable result but for the growing consumer demand for low-cost travel following the world recession, and pressure from national governments to hold prices down so that the valuable contribution of tourist receipts to the state's economy would be in no way impaired.

And finally, these problems were further compounded by price competition within the airline industry itself, as the major airlines sought to maintain their load factors against a background of static demand. The airlines particularly felt the competition of charter airlines led by Laker Airways in the United Kingdom, who broke up existing price cartel for flights along the North Atlantic routes and in doing so, set in motion, a worldwide re-appraisal of the economics of world air travel.

So although air traffic has remained reasonably strong, much is now being carried on at an uneconomic rate. The state airlines already face such difficulties in having to operate routes which are not financially viable as a service to their state, and national governments also intervene to guard sovereign rights over select routes. The sum result has been a sharp fall in the profitability of the world airline system since 1978, with a zero profit in 1979, and a fall of 1.6% (£1,000 million dollars) in 1980.

Table 127. Financial Results: Total IATA Members 1976-1980 — All Services

(million dollars)	1976	1977	1978	1979	1980[1]
Revenues	34,600	39,700	45,000	50,100	60,800
Expenses	33,400	38,100	43,100	50,100	61,800
Balance	+ 1,200	+ 1,600	+ 1,900	-	- 1,000

Source: ICAO Digest of Statistics / Financial Data and IATA Survey
Note: 1 Preliminary figures

The sum result was a shortfall of £500 million in 1980 between operating receipts and costs. This was worse for the main airlines in the International Air Transport Association, which as shown below includes most of the major world airlines, with the exception of Pan-Am, and does indicate the competition from smaller, charter operations.

Table 128. Financial Results: Total World Airlines* 1976-1980 — All Services

(million dollars)	1976	1977	1978	1979	1980[1]
Revenues	43,400	50,344	58,769	70,755	87,500
Expenses	41,244	47,715	55,669	70,019	88,000
Balance	+ 2,156	+ 2,628	+ 3,100	+ 736	- 500

Source: ICAO
Notes: [1] Preliminary figures   * Excludes China, and domestic travel in USSR

Figures on world air passenger movement are generally expressed in terms of "passenger kilometres", the most comparable base because it relates the number of passengers with the distance flown. It is more useful than considering the number of passengers carried when evaluating total world movements, although figures on passengers carried are included below for the main air lines and arrivals by country so they can be compared with the total tourist arrivals in Chapter Two.

In 1980, total passenger kilometres flown amounted to 1,177,600 on all scheduled and non-scheduled flights, whether domestic or international. This was a negligible increase of under 1% over 1979, and followed previous growth rates of around 10% per annum. The performance for international air travel was slightly better than this, showing a 2% increase on all international flights, but this again was a poor showing in comparison with previous trends.

Table 129. World Air Transport Operations 1976-1980

('000 passenger kilometres flown)	1976	1977	1978	1979	1980[1]
International	401.9	439.0	497.1	550.7	562.0
Domestic	476.2	501.7	564.8	620.9	615.6
Total	878.1	940.7	1,061.9	1,171.6	1,177.6

Source: ICAO / IATA

Information on the performance of main international airline routes is available for IATA members, whose scheduled services accounted for 60% of the total international passenger traffic. In 1980, the "load factor" (the percentage of available seats filled) for these airlines was just over 60%, which represented a fall from the 1979 ratio of 63%. Prior to 1980, the load factor had been steadily improving.

Overall, the passenger kilometres flown among these airlines increased by only 3% over the previous year. Looking at the progress of various routes, we can see that the largest route is the North Atlantic, which accounted for 25% of all passenger kilometres flown in 1980. The other main routes were Europe-Middle East (10%) and routes within Europe (12.5%).

None of these routes showed particularly good progress in 1980. Routes within Europe fell by 1.7% over 1979, and the others only showed small increases. Looking at the longer term trend — back to 1976 — we can see that the European routes have been gradually falling as a percentage of the whole; they had a 13.6% market share in 1976.

Routes from Europe to regions outside the continent have also fared badly, although there was a 12% increase in traffic to North Africa from Europe. Europe-Middle East routes were down 7% following several years of promising growth.

The major growth areas involved routes to, and within the Far East and South America, and looking at the five year trends, we can see that there is an expansion of air travel in these developing areas at the expense of the more established routes.

The North Atlantic routes account for one quarter of passenger kilometres flown, so a closer look at this operation would seem useful, particularly as figures are available on the types of tickets sold on North Atlantic flights. They show that types of fares such as Normal Economy and Excursions have given way to Apex and Super Apex fares, while budget/stand-by tickets have grown to account for 6% of the total sold.

To conclude this section, I have summarised trends in the numbers of passengers carried on the major international airlines, and the number of passengers carried by country. The latter figures refer to the country of origin of the airline, and are therefore more useful in showing the relative strengths of countries in the world airline industry than in air passenger movement. Adding up all the passengers carried internationally over the last five years on scheduled flights, the following trend emerges as to the total proportion of international tourists carried by air.

Table 130. Types of Fares Sold on North Atlantic Routes 1976-1980

	1976	1977	1978	1979	1980
Concorde	-	-	1.2%	1.2%	1.4%
First Class	5.4%	5.7%	4.7%	4.8%	4.7%
Economy Normal	24.2%	25.8%	22.0%	20.2%	20.9%
Excursion Regular	32.4%	25.2%	17.9%	14.1%	13.5%
APEX	11.1%	16.9%	19.0%	19.4%	22.1%
SUPER APEX	-	-	8.4%	17.2%	18.2%
G.I.T.	8.4%	8.5%	5.4%	4.2%	3.8%
Budget/Standy-by	-	-	6.0%	6.0%	5.5%
Affinity	2.9%	1.6%	0.9%	0.9%	0.9%
Youth	3.6%	3.2%	1.9%	1.2%	1.0%
Other	12.0%	13.2%	12.6%	10.9%	8.1%
Total	100.0%	100.0%	100.0%	100.0%	100.0%

Source: IATA

Table 131. International Airline Routes

Passenger kilometres flown (million)	1976	1977	1978	1979	1980
North America - South America	9,466	10,507	11,503	9,081	10,496
North America - Central America	10,909	11,041	12,529	13,398	15,652
North Atlantic	62,796	66,750	82,403	85,568	85,463
Mid Atlantic	9,359	10,686	12,642	10,172	10,305
South Atlantic	7,453	7,655	8,807	9,689	10,783
Europe - North Africa	7,142	8,237	8,752	8,268	9,505
Europe - Southern Africa	12,572	13,035	14,996	15,724	16,428
Europe - Middle East	15,695	20,249	22,823	22,470	20,925
Europe - Far East	39,586*	43,533*	31,401	32,773	33,521
Europe - S.W. Pacific			14,863	19,925	18,573
Middle East - Far East			2,569	4,857	5,932
Africa - Far East			1,113	1,264	1,398
North & Mid-Pacific	15,732	16,446	20,680	14,135	13,891
South Pacific	6,614	6,551	7,064	5,866	6,135
Within North America	4,882	5,039	5,155	6,333	6,512
Within Central America	370	494	309	322	344
With South America	1,555	1,670	2,019	2,481	3,135
Within Europe	34,861	37,553	39,738	42,960	42,231
Within Africa	1,345	1,224	1,291	1,512	1,609
Within Middle East	3,856	5,230	5,776	5,661	5,779
Within Far East & S.W. Pacific	9,482	10,035	11,646	13,175	16,210
Other	2,615	3,443	2,001	2,360	2,684
Total	256,290	279,378	320,080	327,994	337,511

Source: IATA
Notes: * Europe - Far East & Australasia

Table 132. Proportion of Total World Tourist Trips Carried on Scheduled Airlines

('000s)	Passengers Carried by Scheduled Services (International)	Total World Tourist Trips	% on Scheduled Airlines
1976	118,500	294,000	40
1977	128,000	312,000	41
1978	142,000	324,000	44
1979	158,000	346,000	46
1980	161,000	355,000	45

Source: ICAO / Own Calculations

In **Western Europe**, the most significant carrier is the United Kingdom, which accounted for a quarter of all passengers carried by the European airlines in 1980. There were no less than 15 airlines operating in the U.K., but British Airways took the lion's share and was by far the largest European airline ahead of Air France and Lufthansa. These three accounted for 40% of the European total in 1980. British Airways and Air France are the two largest airlines in the world in terms of passengers carried internationally. A meagre 4% of world travel was accounted for by the airlines of **Eastern Europe**, where the major presence was the Russian airline, Aeroflot, with a one third share.

U.S. airlines naturally dominate the scene in North and Central America, which has about 20% of the world's total traffic. The U.S.A. has 18 airlines flying internationally led by non-IATA member, Pan-Am, with a 30% share. The second main airline in the region is in fact Air Canada, accounting for 17% of passengers carried by airlines in this region.

Airlines in **South America** contribute only 4% of the world's total international market. No single airline dominates but Varig (Brazil) and Aerolineas Argentina are prominent.

The **North Africa and Middle East** region has a significant international presence with an 8% overall share. This is split between a number of airlines which carry 1 million or more passengers including Air Algerie, El Al (Israel), Alia (Jordan) and Kuwait Airlines. But well ahead of all these is Saudi Arabian airlines, which has shown tremendous growth and now carried almost 2.5 billion passengers — 18% of the regions total.

The pattern in **Africa** is fragmented with a large number of airlines carrying

Regional Traffic Shares of IATA Scheduled Passenger Traffic

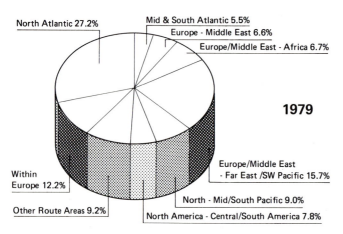

North Atlantic 27.2%
Mid & South Atlantic 5.5%
Europe - Middle East 6.6%
Europe/Middle East - Africa 6.7%

1979

Europe/Middle East - Far East /SW Pacific 15.7%

Within Europe 12.2%

North - Mid/South Pacific 9.0%

Other Route Areas 9.2%

North America - Central/South America 7.8%

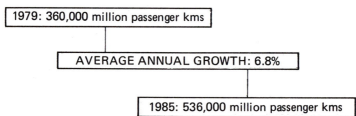

1979: 360,000 million passenger kms

AVERAGE ANNUAL GROWTH: 6.8%

1985: 536,000 million passenger kms

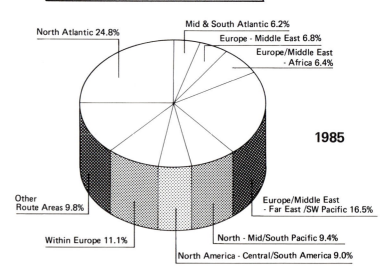

North Atlantic 24.8%
Mid & South Atlantic 6.2%
Europe - Middle East 6.8%
Europe/Middle East - Africa 6.4%

1985

Other Route Areas 9.8%

Europe/Middle East - Far East /SW Pacific 16.5%

Within Europe 11.1%

North - Mid/South Pacific 9.4%

North America - Central/South America 9.0%

international passengers. Standing out in size and growth is Egypt Air, carrying 1.3 billion passengers in 1980.

The **Far East** contributes about 12% to the international market. 22% of this is accounted for by Japan's two airlines, with Singapore Airlines holding a further 19%. Several other airlines in the region carry in excess of 1 billion passengers including KAL (Korea), Air India, MAS (Malaysia), PIA (Pakistan and Thai Airways (Thailand).

Two airlines dominate in **Oceania**; Quantas (Australia) with a 60% share, and Air New Zealand, with a further 33%. The Oceanic region only contributes 2% to the world international passenger traffic.

To summarise, the leading airline in the world in terms of international passengers carried is British Airways, and seven other European airlines appear among the "top ten". In terms of national totals, the U.S.A. leads with a 15% overall share followed by the United Kingdom with an 11% share. No other countries come close, because the large number of airlines within these countries give them a powerful overall presence.

1980 is of course only one year, and follows several years of rapid growth. So what will the future bring? I have produced my own forecasts of world tourist growth in the final Chapter of this study, and these are fairly optimistic. So the airline industry will certainly be able to find comfort in a continued growth in international tourism. Also, without doubt, the proportion of tourist trips which incorporate air travel will also increase. The main problems are likely to be economic; the airlines will have to come to some agreement about pricing in order to be able to sustain present load factors, a less rapid level of passenger growth, the effects of further increases in energy costs and the costs of further investment for expansion.

IATA themselves have produced forecasts of passenger kilometres which they expect will be flown up to 1985. Their overall figures seem optimistic, particularly when their estimate for 1980 (the figures were calculated based on 1979 actuals) showed a 5.7% growth against the actual growth of 2.9%. But their overall growth of 7.3% per annum does not look wholly unreasonable. I think we can conclude that the rate of increase will recover to between 5-7% per annum.

Table 133. The Top Twenty Airlines in 1980*

	Passengers Carried Internationally	
	Millions	%
British Airways	12,084	7.5%
Air France	9,074	5.6%
Pan Am	7,868	4.9%
Lufthansa	7,458	4.6%
Swissair	5,221	3.2%
Iberia	5,130	3.2%
SAS	4,740	2.9%
Air Canada	4,243	2.6%
Alitalia	4,175	2.6%
KLM	3,849	2.4%
Singapore	3,827	2.4%
Japan	3,680	2.3%
Eastern	3,299	2.0%
American	2,954	1.8%
Cathay Pacific	2,783	1.7%
TWA	2,739	1.7%
Aeroflot	2,503	1.6%
Saudi Arabian	2,347	1.5%
Korean Airlines	2,105	1.3%
Quantas	1,961	1.2%
Others		43.3%
Total	161,000	100.0%

Source: Own Calculations from ICAO
Note: * Based on the criteria stated.

Table 134.

IATA INTERNATIONAL SCHEDULED PASSENGER TRAFFIC 1979-1985
Passenger-Kilometres (thousand million) and Annual Growth Rates

Region	Actual 1979	1980	1981	Forecast 1982	1983	1984	1985	Forecast Average Annual Growth Rate 1979-1985
U.S.-Europe	84.0	89.0+ 6.0%	91.7+ 3.0%	97.2+ 6.0%	103.0+ 6.0%	109.2+ 6.0%	115.8+ 6.0%	+ 5.5%
Canada-Europe	13.9	13.9+ 0	14.3+ 3.0%	15.0+ 5.0%	15.8+ 5.0%	16.6+ 5.0%	17.4+ 5.0%	+ 3.8%
Mid-Atlantic	10.2	10.9+ 7.0%	11.9+ 9.0%	13.0+ 9.0%	14.2+ 9.0%	15.5+ 9.0%	16.9+ 9.0%	+ 8.7%
South Atlantic	9.7	10.4+ 7.0%	11.1+ 7.0%	12.2+ 10.0%	13.4+ 10.0%	14.7+ 10.0%	16.2+ 10.0%	+ 8.9%
Europe Middle E.	23.8	25.0+ 5.0%	26.8+ 7.0%	28.9+ 8.0%	31.2+ 8.0%	33.7+ 8.0%	36.4+ 8.0%	+ 7.3%
Europe/Middle E. S. Africa	10.7	11.2+ 5.0%	11.9+ 6.0%	12.6+ 6.0%	13.4+ 6.0%	14.2+ 6.0%	15.1+ 6.0%	+ 5.9%
Europe/Middle E. W. Africa	8.1	8.3+ 3.0%	8.7+ 5.0%	9.2+ 6.0%	9.8+ 6.0%	10.4+ 6.0%	11.0+ 6.0%	+ 5.2%
Europe/Middle E. Rest of Africa	5.3	5.7+ 7.0%	6.2+ 8.0%	6.7+ 8.0%	7.2+ 8.0%	7 8+ 8.0%	8.4+ 8.0%	+ 7.9%
Europe/Middle E.- Far East	36.7	38.5+ 5.0%	41.6+ 8.0%	45.3+ 9.0%	49.4+ 9.0%	53.8+ 9.0%	58.6+ 9.0%	+ 8.1%
Europe/Middle E. S.W.Pacific	19.9	20.9+ 5.0%	21.9+ 5.0%	23.7+ 8.0%	25.6+ 8.0%	27.6+ 8.0%	29.8+ 8.0%	+ 6.9%
North Mid Pacific	23.9	25.3+ 6.0%	27.1+ 7.0%	29.3+ 8.0%	31.6+ 8.0%	34.1+ 8.0%	36.8+ 8.0%	+ 7.4%
South Pacific	8.6	9.5+ 10.0%	10.0+ 5.0%	10.8+ 8.0%	11 7+ 8.0%	12.6+ 8.0%	13.6+ 8.0%	+ 7.9%
N.America-Central America	14.5	16.1+ 11.0%	17.7+ 10.0%	19.3+ 9.0%	21.0+ 9.0%	22.9+ 9.0%	25.0+ 9.0%	+ 9.5%
N.America-S.America	13.6	15.2+ 12.0%	16.7+ 10.0%	18.2+ 9.0%	19.8+ 9.0%	21.6+ 9.0%	23.5+ 9.0%	+ 9.4%
Within Europe	43.8	44.7+ 2.0%	46.9+ 5.0%	49.7+ 6.0%	52.7+ 6.0%	55.9+ 6.0%	59.3+ 6.0%	+ 5.1%
Within Far East/ S.W.Pacific	13.2	14.5+ 10.0%	16 0+ 10.0%	17.4+ 9.0%	19.0+ 9.0%	20.7+ 9.0%	22.6+ 9.0%	+ 9.3%
Other Route/Areas	19.9	21.3+ 7.0%	22.8+ 7.0%	24.4+ 7.0%	26.1+ 7.0%	27.9+ 7.0%	29.9+ 7.0%	+ 6.9%
TOTAL IATA International	359.8	380.4+ 5.7%	403.3+ 6.0%	423.9+ 7.3%	464.9+ 7.3%	499.2+ 7.3%	536.3+ 7.4%	+ 6.8%

NB.   Pan American World Airways contributed to these forecasts and is included in the data base
The percentage points included in the period averages and the growth rates for tota. IATA internati nal traffic are the result of statistical
aggregatio., and are not intended to show accuracy.

Table 135.
Western Europe

PASSENGERS CARRIED ON INTERNATIONAL SCHEDULED AIRLINES 1976-1980

	1976	1977	1978	1979	1980
Austria	1,041	1,117	1,219	1,283	1,267
Belgium	1,682	1,839	1,976	2,043	1,974
Cyprus	225	266	315	387	441
Denmark	1,175	1,226	1,303	1,403	1,354
Finland	698	719	790	922	969
France	7,815	8,742	9,701	10,232	9,952
W. Germany	5,752	6,087	6,556	7,285	7,458
Greece	1,159	1,156	1,338	1,541	1,563
Iceland	402	406	452	453	300
Ireland	1,436	1,501	1,606	1,783	1,636
Italy	3,743	4,331	4,305	3,750	4,193
Luxembourg	250e	260e	290e	300e	162e
Malta	221	255	352	382	401
Monaco	30	34	38	43	44e
Netherlands	3,706	4,095	4,377	4,598	4,633
Norway	1,175	1,226	1,303	1,403	1,354
Portugal	754	842	950	1,099	971
Spain	4,082	4,545	5,016	5,167	5,137
Sweden	1,763	1,838	1,954	2,105	2,031
Switzerland	4,497	4,789	4,988	5,181	5,221
Turkey	584	595	584	626e	377e
UK	13,403	13,945	16,753	18,239	18,256
TOTAL					

Source: IACO/IATA.

Table 136.   PASSENGERS CARRIED ON INTERNATIONAL
SCHEDULED AIRLINES 1976-1980
Eastern Europe

TO FROM	1976	1977	1978	1979	1980
Bulgaria	400e	420e	450e	485e	486e
Czechoslovakia	490	522	548	604	585
Hungary	427	555	659	830	858
Poland	729	824	936	1,000	931
Romania	258	298	368	382	383
USSR	2,043	2,199	2,407	2,651	2,503
Yugoslavia	1,098	1,210	1,393	1,139	969
TOTAL					

Source: IACO/IATA

Table 137.   PASSENGERS CARRIED ON INTERNATIONAL
SCHEDULED AIRLINES 1976-1980
North & Central America

	1976	1977	1978	1979	1980
Bahamas	120e	122e	128e	146e	160e
Barbados	34	42	50	54	46
Canada	4,132	4,335	4,559	5,391	5,532
Costa Rica	222	238	263	328	332
Cuba	77	90	116	183	120
Dominican Rep.	363	393	401	451	466
Guatemala	119	138	136	156	119
Honduras	230	244	260	292	325
Jamaica	621	533	637	731	660
Mexico	1,436	1,562	2,009	3,470	2,777
Nicaragua	49e	50e	50e	80e	50e
Panama	273	256	269	292	303
Trinidad & Tobago	384	477	254	514	633
USA	17,655	18,955	20,808	24,427	25,723
TOTAL					

Source: IACO/IATA

Table 138.   PASSENGERS CARRIED ON INTERNATIONAL SCHEDULED AIRLINES 1976-1980

South America

	1976	1977	1978	1979	1980
Argentina	639	817	929	1,146	1,293
Bolivia	139	162	187	261	268
Brazil	948	985	1,059	1,216	1,330
Colombia	550	638	660	766	753
Chile	218	237	223	235	299
Ecuador	110	159	193	228	250
El Salvador	170	211	225	258	265
Paraguay	50	88	95	100	109
Peru	138	127	167	217	221
Suriname	30e	33e	90e	123e	120e
Uruguay	263	233	224	383	433
Venezuela	629	737	843	933	947
TOTAL	3,894	4,439	4,907	5,881	6,308

Source: IACO/IATA

146

**Table 139.   PASSENGERS CARRIED ON INTERNATIONAL
SCHEDULED AIRLINES 1976-1980**

North Africa & Middle East

	1976	1977	1978	1979	1980
Algeria	1,050	1,058	1,129	1,413	1,500
Bahrain	240	300	375	457	522
Iran	741	918	1,027	525	396
Iraq	367	496	519	531	434
Israel	902	1,039	1,090	1,154	1,043
Jordan	400	536	696	875	1,070
Kuwait	737	812	849	965	1,076
Lebanon	1,050	928	863	904	930
Libya	334	368	395	400	468
Morocco	695	912	979	982	906
Oman	240	300	375	457	522
Qatar	240	300	375	457	522
Saudi Arabia	1,040	1,327	1,718	2,291	2,348
Syria	352	376	432	371	383
Tunisia	725	775	877	981	898
U.A.R.	240	300	375	457	522
Yemen, Rep	220	230	250	250	255
Yemen, Dem	78	82	88	92	94
TOTAL	9,651	11,057	12,412	13,562	13,889

Source: IACO/IATA.

Table 140.   PASSENGERS CARRIED ON INTERNATIONAL SCHEDULED AIRLINES 1976-1980

Africa

	1976	1977	1978	1979	1980
Angola	31	33	38	39	51
Benin	40	45	52	57	61
Botswana	6	8	8	10	20
Burundi	4e	5e	5e	6e	11e
Cameroon	68	104	108	112	126
Central African Rep.	40	45	52	57	61
Chad	40	45	52	57	61
Comoros e	12	15	18	22	25
Congo	40	45	57	63	67
Egypt	812	959	992	1,122	1,270
Ethiopia	145	147	137	153	186
Gambia e	38	47	55	62	65
Ghana	101	121	169	171	175
Ivory Coast	40	45	52	57	61
Kenya	399	104	190	190	204
Lesotho	6	7	8	9	10e
Liberia	1	1	2	2	2
Madagascar	63	62	66	63	46
Malawi	65	71	71	66	52
Mali	40	43	37	41	42
Mauritius	33	26	50	75	77
Mozambique	40	42	42	39	52
Niger	40	45	52	57	61
Nigeria	105	179	210	229	301
Senegal	77	85	92	97	71
Seychelles	7	8	10	12	15
S. Africa	603	666	745	809	801
Sudan	165	237	26	270	311
Swaziland	14e	15e	16e	30e	31e
Tanzania	207	13	43	62	94
Togo	44	49	56	61	65
Uganda	69	67	66	60	60
Upper Volta	40	45	52	57	65
Zaire	87	102	94	102	92
Zambia	87	121	109	106	114
TOTAL	1,538	1,557	1,495	1,892	2,173

Source: IACO/IATA

Table 141. **PASSENGERS CARRIED ON INTERNATIONAL SCHEDULED AIRLINES 1976-1980**

Far East

	1976	1977	1978	1979	1980
Afghanistan	81	90	78	70	51
Bangladesh	86	121	173	243	270
Burma	46	50	55	60	64
China	150e	160e	240e	319e	360e
India	923	1,221	1,348	1,459	1,668
Indonesia	524	653	728	748	922
Japan	2,751	3,414	3,921	4,360	4,499
Korea (S)	1,291	1,385	1,660	1,933	2,105
Laos	15	12e	12	13	13
Malaysia	973	1,149	1,317	1,396	1,822
Maldives	10e	13e	20e	25e	27e
Nepal	68e	80e	85e	175	173e
Pakistan	786	1,049	1,179	1,286	1,501
Philippines	400	517	620	732	997
Singapore	2,132	2,497	2,893	3,377	3,827
Sri Lanka	101	140	63	60	235
Thailand	1,337	994	1,383	1,594	1,924
TOTAL					

Source: IACO/IATA

Table 142. **PASSENGERS CARRIED ON INTERNATIONAL SCHEDULED AIRLINES 1976-1980**

Oceania

	1976	1977	1978	1979	1980
Australia	1,564	1,552	1,631	1,891	1,961
Fiji	68e	75e	90e	105e	90e
New Zealand	766	834	910	1,001	1,041
Papua New Guinea	27	80	88	96	99
TOTAL					

Source: IACO/IATA

149

Table 143.   PASSENGERS CARRIED BY AIRLINE 1976-1980

'000's	International Scheduled Airlines	1976	1977	1978	1979	1980
Afghanistan	Ariana	81	90	75	70	51
Algeria	Air Algerie		1,058	1,130	1,413	1,500
Angola	Taag	56	34	35e	39	51
Argentina	Aerolineas Argentina	554	717	824	1,059	992
Argentina	Austral	84	101	105	88	4
Australia	Qantas	1,564	1,552	1,631	1,891	1,961
Austria	Aua	1,041	1,117	1,219	1,283	1,267
Bangladesh	Biman	86	121	173	243	270
Barbados	Caribbean Airways	34	42	50	54	42
Belgium	Sabena	1,682	1,839	1,976	2,043	1,974
Bolivia	Lab	139	162	187	261	268
Brazil	Cruzeiro	245	248	269	343	411
Brazil	Varig	703	738	790	873	919
Canada	Air Canada	3,108	3,263	3,421	4,164	4,243
Canada	CP Air	886	878	926	947	942
Canada	Nordair	27	30	35	45	77
Canada	Pacific Western	110	164	177	236	234
Central African Empire	Air Afrique	45	47	52	57	56
Chile	Ladeco (domestic)		3	556	18	36
Chile	Lan Chile	218	234	225	217	263
Colombia	Aerocondor	117	135	159	142	145
Colombia	Avianca	397	443	449	575	699
Colombia	Sam	37	56	53	49	46
Costa Rica	Lacsa	222	238	263	328	332
Cuba	Cubana	77	81	119	183	120
Cyprus	Cyprus Airways	225	266	315	388	441
Czechoslovakia	CSA	490	522	548	604	585
Dominican Rep.	Aerovias Quisqueyana	65	55	9	-	-
Dominican Rep.	CDA		339	392	386	390
Dominican Rep.	Aerolin Dominicanas		12	12	15	20
Ecuador	Ecuatoriana		159	193	228	250

Continued/.......

Table 143 continued ......

'000's	International Scheduled Airlines	1976	1977	1978	1979	1980
Egypt	Egyptair	812	959	1,005	1,122	1,270
El Salvador	Taca		211	225	258	243
Ethiopia	Ethiopian	144	147	137	153	186
Finland	Finnair	698	719	790	922	969
France	Air France	7,135	7,990	8,854	9,382	9,074
France	UTA	560	752	848	851	878
Germany, W.	Lufthansa	5,752	6,087	6,556	7,285	7,458
Ghana	Ghanair		121	171	171	175
Greece	Olympic	1,159	1,156	1,339	1,541	1,563
Guatemala	Aviateca	119	138	136	156	119
Gulf States	Gulf Air	960	1,199	1,498	1,700e	1,750e
Honduras	Sahsa		171	181	192	68
Honduras	Tan	69	73	79	100	42
Hungary	Malev	427	555	659	830	787
Iceland	Flugfelag	111	134	141	205	300
Iceland	Loftleidir	292	272	311	248	260e
India	Air India	789	1,036	1,107	1,148	1,350
India	Indian Airlines	135	185	243	311	318
Indonesia	Garuda	500	628	714	729	916
Indonesia	Merpati Nusantara	24	25	25	18	20e
Iran	Iran Air	741	920	994	525	396
Iraq	Iraqi	371	498	524	531	434
Ireland	Aer Lingus	1,435	1,512	1,606	1,783	1,636
Israel	El Al	902	1,039	1,090	1,154	1,043
Italy	Alisarda	9	9	12	13	15
Italy	Alitalia	3,734	3,606	3,922	3,738	4,175
Jamaica	Air Jamaica	621	533	637	731	660
Japan	Jal	2,529	3,021	3,484	3,895	3,680
Japan	Japan Asia Airways	222	394	437	466	518
Jordan	Alia	439	518	690	848	1,070
Kenya	Kenya Airways		104	190	190	204
Kuwait	Kuwait Airways	737	812	850	965	856
Lebanon	Meal		929	863	904	710

Continued/.........

Table 143 continued ......

'000's	International Scheduled Airlines	1976	1977	1978	1979	1980
Libya	Libyan Arab Airlines	334	357	395	400	468
Madagascar	Air Madagascar	63	62	64	63	23
Malawi	Air Malawi	65	71	65	66	52
Malaysia	MAS	973	1,149	1,317	1,396	1,822
Mali	Air Mali		43	37	41	42
Malta	Air Malta	221	255	352	382	402
Mauritius	Air Mauritius		26	50e	75	77
Mexico	Aeromexico	595	590	734	789	597
Mexico	Mexicana	840	951	1,271	2,680	1,782
Morocco	Royal Air Maroc	675	890	955	957	906
Mozambique	Deta	65	42	42	39	52
Netherlands	ALM	280	355	360e	120	235
Netherlands	KLM	3,251	3,580	3,759	3,927	3,849
Netherlands	NLM	203	196	188	241	315
New Zealand	Air New Zealand	755	804	910	1,001	1,041
Nigeria	Nigeria Airways	125	120	214	229	200
Pakistan	PIA	751	1,048	1,179	1,286	1,501
Panama	Air Panama	160	143	152	164	140
Panama	Copa	113	113	117	129	104
Papua New Guinea	Air Niugini	72	80	88	96	99
Peru	Aeroperu	138	127	168	209	196
Peru	Faucett	-	-	-	8	25
Philippines	PAL	438	517	621	732	997
Poland	LOT	729	825	936	1,000	931
Portugal	TAP	754	842	950	1,099	971
Republic of Korea	KAP	1,145	1,385	1,660	1,933	2,105
Romania	Tarom	258	298	368	382	383
Saudi Arabia	Saudi Arabian	1,040	1,327	1,718	2,291	2,347
Scandinavia	SAS	4,114	4,290	4,559	4,911	4,740
Sierra Leone	Sierra Leone		18	18e	25e	26e
Singapore	SIA	2,132	2,497	2,893	3,378	3,827

Continued/.........

Table 143 continued ......

'000's	International Scheduled Airlines	1976	1977	1978	1979	1980
South Africa	SAA	603	666	745	809	802
Spain	Aviaco	5	6	8	8	7
Spain	Iberia	4,021	4,539	5,009	5,159	5,130
Sri Lanka	Air Lanka	101	140	63	41	216
Sudan	Sudanair	219	237	250e	270	311
Switzerland	Swissair	4,497	4,789	4,988	5,181	5,221
Syria	Syrian Arab	475	377	432	371	383
Tanzania	Air Tanzania		13	43	62	94
Thailand	TAC	32	26	51	67	73
Thailand	Thai International	906	968	1,332	1,527	1,692
Trinidad & Tobago	BWIA	384	477	254	514	633
Tunisia	Tunis Air	725	775	877	981	771
Turkey	THY	584	595	584	626e	377e
USSR	Aeroflot	1,943	2,199	2,405	2,651	2,503
UK	Air Anglia	162	216	236	264	250e
UK	Air Wales		6e	7	7e	7e
UK	Air Westward		5e	5	5e	5e
UK	Aurigny	185	217	222	235e	230e
UK	BIA	182	221	230	368	350e
UK	British Airferries	151	174	178	180e	170e
UK	British Airways	9,610	9,596	11,300	12,530	12,084
UK	British Caledonian	654	773	889	1,004	1,136
UK	British Midland	77	88	97	107	82
UK	Brymon Airways	6	7	7	7e	7e
UK	Cathay Pacific	1,567	1,796	2,230	2,547	2,783
UK	Dan-Air	139	164	186	219	195
UK	Haywards Aviation		1	1	1	1
UK	Intra Airways	42	45	59	65e	60e
UK	Laker		55	264	302	728
UR Cameroon	Cameroon Airlines	84	104	108	112e	126e
USA	Allegheny	432	436	362	400e	390e
USA	American Airlines	1,211	2,197	2,561	2,915	2,954

Table 143 continued ......

'000's	International Scheduled Airlines	1976	1977	1978	1979	1980
USA	Braniff	818	897	1,292	1,604	1,819
USA	Continental		9	58	127	205
USA	Delta	680	727	825	980	1,127
USA	Eastern	2,416	2,498	2,694	3,229	3,299
USA	Frontier	32	36	31	113	151
USA	Hughes Air West	236	286	270	273	311
USA	National	98	146	249	332	230
USA	North Central	216	236	218	126	120e
USA	Northwest	1,254	1,257	809	1,520	1,811
USA	Pan Am	6,109	6,466	7,170	7,812	7,868
USA	Southern	40	43	50	30	30e
USA	Texas International	124	97	116	246	391
USA	TWA	2,053	2,190	2,679	2,939	2,739
USA	United	427	389	374	300	317
USA	Western	898	1,012	1,178	1,309	1,369
USA	Wien Air Alaska	15	9	14	15	11
Uruguay	ARCO	50	51	50	66	89
Uruguay	Pluna	213	182	175	180e	344
Venezuela	LAV	70	100	126	126	48
Venezuela	Viasa	559	638	717	808	422
Yugoslavia	JAT	869	1,210	1,393	676	969
Zaire	Air Zaire	88	102	92	72	91
Zambia	Zambia Airways		121	109	106	114
TOTAL						

Source: IATA, ICAO Statistical Yearbook.

CAR RENTAL

As international air transport has expanded, so has the demand for car rental, and this demand has built into a worldwide industry. Many tourists arriving by air, particularly business visitors, rent cars at airports for use in the country visited. So the car rental industry is very dependent on the air travel industry, which is itself dependent on trends in world tourists.

The worldwide car rental industry is worth about $7,000 million, and two-thirds of this is estimated to come from car rental offices at airlines. The world demand can be very roughly split as follows:-

North America	50%
Europe	30%
Other	20%
Total	100%

The market is dominated by the two large U.S. firms, Hertz and Avis. Hertz operates in 120 countries from 4,000 outlets and has a fleet of 300,000 cars, while Avis has 3,500 outlets in 100 countries, and a fleet size of about one quarter of a million.

In 1981, a merger by Europcar and Godfrey Davis created a third main group within the world structure. Europcar are the leading car rental firm in Europe with a particularly strong presence in France, Italy and Switzerland. Godfrey Davis are the market leaders in the United Kingdom, which is Europe's largest market. The new combine should be an extremely competitive world contender, and undoubtedly lead in Europe as a whole.

CHAPTER SIX
DIRECTION OF TRAVEL

In Chapter Four of this study, we looked at the total number of arrivals in countries throughout the world, arranged into our eight standard regions. Now, using these regional breakdowns again, we shall consider the source of this tourist intake in terms of region and country of origin.

This is an important factor in the marketing and promotion of tourism, and therefore extremely relevant to the travel industry. Knowledge about the types of visitors assists in the provision of the most suitable types of facilities in terms of hotels, catering facilities, sports facilities and so forth. And it is also important for targeting overseas advertising and promotional activity.

We shall look at tourist intake by nationality in two ways; firstly, using our eight regional breakdowns, we shall consider the regional source of tourists entering each country surveyed. Then we shall analyse tourist consumption in terms of the major travelling nations.

The figures in this section are presented in percentages, and generally refer to 1979, the latest year for which complete figures are available. I have presented the figures in percentages because of the discrepancies in the methods by which figures are collected in different countries — some refer to arrivals by country of origin, some nights spent in accommodation, stays in hotels etc. They may not be strictly compatible in some instances, but they are the best we have, and certainly offer a broad and useful guide to the direction of travel.

The analysis by region immediately shows that most people stay within their region of origin when travelling "abroad". In fact, most of the major travelling nations are surrounded by a catchment area which takes a sizeable proportion of the overseas travellers from that country. In Western Europe, this is the Mediterranean, in North America, the Caribbean. So however international travel is, it is worth noting this strong level of regional retention.

In **Western Europe**, at least 70% of tourists visiting the countries in the region do so from other countries within the region. France, for example receives 86% of its visitors from other West European countries, while Spain receives over 90% from either Western or Eastern Europe. The other main consumers of travellers from the Eastern bloc — in proportion to their total intake — are Greece and Italy.

The second main area of visitors to Western Europe is The Americas. Travellers from the Americas have most impact on more Northerly European countries such as Norway, Belgium and West Germany, falling to limited proportions towards the south. The other regions contribute negligible proportions to the West European intake, although the Far East has some presence in Holland, West Germany and Switzerland.

The second analysis for West Europe, by major countries, reveals that this tendency towards proximity extends towards neighbouring countries. Three-fifths of the visitors to Austria are West Germans; the Spanish account for two-thirds of all tourists in Portugal, and 80% of visitors to Jersey are British. Of the major travelling nations outside Europe, the Japanese make most impact on Switzerland and West Germany, and the Americans on Norway, Ireland and again, West Germany.

Visitors to countries in **Eastern Europe** come almost exclusively from either West or Eastern Europe. With the exception of Yugoslavia, which demonstrates a high proportion of visitors from the West, the most open countries are Bulgaria and U.S.S.R. The latter is the only country to display a significant non-European intake due to visitors from the Far East.

A large number of visitors to countries in **North and Central America** come from Canada and the U.S.A., so the proportion of tourist consumption to this region from this region is again high. This applies to both large and small countries; Canada and the U.S.A. themselves receive, respectively, 87% and 74% of tourists from their own region. Small Caribbean islands such as British Virgin Islands and Bermuda receive over 90% of their total intake from the North American region.

Tourists from Europe thus form quite small proportions in North America, although the more recent availability of low-cost travel will have increased their numbers. In 1979, Grenada, Guadeloupe and Martinique were most open to travellers from Western Europe, South Americans contribute significant proportions in the more southerly countries, but the intake from other regions is extremely low.

Tourists from the States form an important proportion of all visitors to their neighbouring countries in the North and Central American area. They account for over 80% of visitors to Mexico, Canada and Bermuda. French tourists account for a sizeable percentage of visitors to ex-colonies such as Guadeloupe and Martinique. The British like Trinidad & Tobago, Barbados and Panama.

There are considerable fluctuations in the types of visitors to the countries of **South America**. Visitors from other countries in the same region account for 75-80% of arrivals in Chile, Colombia and Paraguay, but considerably less in Bolivia, Peru and Ecuador. Here, as in Brazil and Venezuela, visitors from Europe form a substantial slice along with the North Americans. South America is popular among the West Germans, the French, and the Swiss, especially Bolivia and Peru.

Visitors from Western Europe form a large proportion of total visitors to **North Africa and the Middle East**, particularly the main North African holiday locations like Tunisia, Algeria and Morocco. This region is unlike the others covered so far, in that the proportion of visitors from the same region is in some instances very small. This is not surprisingly true for Israel, but also true of Morocco, Iran, Tunisia and Yemen. But other countries do receive most of their visitors from their region and considerable contrasts exist.

This is the first region to show a significant level of visitors from Africa; they account for 25% of visitors to Morocco, and Yemen. But European visitors dominate, and are well ahead of North American visitors although the Americans are the main nation visiting Israel, followed by the main West European countries. The European nations, such as Britain, Germany and France also like North Africa, but show less prominently in the Middle East states.

Tourist consumption in **Africa** is the most widely spread of the eight regions under review. Again there are considerable contrasts, with intake from the same region accounting for over 90% of visitors to Botswana, a mere 3% in the Ivory Coast. Visitors from Europe feature prominently in most countries but intake from the Middle East is significant in the more proximate countries and there are sizeable numbers of Far East visitors.

The strength of European presence is in a number of cases due to visitors from one country, mainly due to colonial origins. The French form 30-40% of the visitors to the Ivory Coast, Madagascar and the Congo; the British go to Ghana, Kenya and Malawi, and a perplexing 80% of visitors to Gambia are from Scandinavia. The Seychelles are popular with the British, the French and the Italians. The Belgians head for Zaire.

Countries in the **Far East** region are, like the African nations, open to visitors from a wide number of places. Again, it is a broad region, and visitors from Europe, North America and Oceania, jostle for market share along with the Far East region itself. Visitors from within the region dominate in Macau, Malaysia and Taiwan, but rather less in more developed areas such as Singapore, Hong Kong, India and Japan. These are more open to visitors from further afield, notably Europeans, but also North Americans and Australasians.

The major travelling nations form a substantial proportion of visitors to the Far East. 12% of visitors to Indonesia are Australian. Japan accounts for over 60% of tourist arrivals in South Korea and Taiwan. The British have a strong presence in Pakistan, and India, the French in Sri Lanka. The Americans are generally much in evidence, notably in Japan and the Philippines.

Our final region is **Oceania**. As Australians are major travellers, they travel in large numbers to other countries in the same region, but generally, inter-regional travel is more limited here. Oceania is a popular area for the North Americans, notably Hawaii and French Polynesia and Western European visitors are also prominent in Australia and the New Hebrides. Arrivals from the Far East are also significant. The U.S.A. features prominently in the tourst intake of countries in Oceania. Almost 60% of visitors to Hawaii are from the States, while Japan also features here prominently, and in some of the smaller islands such as New Caledonia. But Australia and New Zealand do account for a sizeable proportion of visitors to the Oceanic region in overall terms.

Overall, then, inter-regional travel accounts for about two-thirds of world tourist intake, and within the regions, countries which are geographically close are more likely to entertain tourists from their neighbours. The regions which least exhibit this tendency are less developed regions which do not contain large travelling nations, but do contain attractive tourist locations, either for holiday or business reasons. The regions most exhibiting this tendency are Africa, and North Africa and the Middle East. This is less true of the Far East and Oceania, because of the presence, respectively, of Japan and Australia within these regions as tourists from these countries increase the level of regional retention.

Apart from these obvious geographical connections, historical factors are also important in the direction of world travel. Countries which were, or are, dependent territories are likely to receive a large number of tourists from the parent nation, and social, linguistic and cultural links may be important too. The other factors — costs, transport, accommodation facilities etc. — are considered elsewhere in this book.

DIRECTION OF TRAVEL — TABLES

The following tables present figures for 1979 on tourist consumption by region, or by country of origin.

The regions are the eight standard regions used throughout this book.

The countries are the main travelling nations.

(1)	Including New Zealand
(2)	Including Luxembourg
(3)	Including Portugal
(4)	Including Austria
(5)	Including Canada
(6)	Including The Netherlands
(7)	Including Eire

Source:	World Tourism Organisation
	O.E.C.D. Tourism Committee
	National Statistical Offices
	National Tourist Offices

Unit: Percentages of Tourist Arrivals, Visits, Stays, or Nights.

Table 144.   DIRECTION OF TOURISM 1979
                         PERCENTAGE BREAKDOWN — REGIONS

Western Europe

TO %	FROM West Europe	East Europe	North & Central America	South America
Austria	88.2	3.3	4.7	0.4
Belgium	——77.0——		12.6	1.9
Cyprus	67.0	1.4	3.4	-
Denmark	——82.4——		9.0	-
Finland	——79.9——		14.9	0.6
France	86.2	0.4	5.2	1.4
W. Germany	70.3	2.9	15.0	2.1
Greece	60.0	12.9	13.1	-
Iceland	64.9	1.3	31.2	-
Ireland	——79.5——		17.0	
Italy	80.5	9.7	4.6	1.0
Jersey	96.9			
Luxembourg	——85.2——		9.8	-
Malta	89.2	0.3	1.9	-
Netherlands	——72.3——		13.3	3.3
Norway	71.8	1.3	19.9	0.8
Portugal	84.3	1.0	7.6	3.5
San Marino	97.9	0.4		
Spain	——91.0——		2.8	0.7
Sweden	74.5	-	12.2	-
Switzerland	——73.2——		12.4	2.6
Turkey	47.0	15.5	11.9	1.2
UK	62.2	1.4	17.6	1.8

Source :WTO/OECD/National Offices.

Middle East & North Africa	Africa	Far East	Oceania	Unknown/Others	Total
0.4	0.3	0.8	0.8	1.1	100.0
—3.8—		—4.7—		-	100.0
19.5	2.0	-	1.3	5.4	100.0
-	-	2.0	-	6.6	100.0
—0.6—		2.8	1.2	-	100.0
2.4	0.5	2.7	0.7	0.5	100.0
—2.3—		6.1	1.2	0.1	100.0
2.5	1.3	2.5	2.6	5.1	100.0
-	-	—1.3—		1.3	100.0
—3.5—				-	100.0
0.2	0.4	0.8	0.9	1.9	100.0
—3.1—				-	100.0
—0.7—		-	-	4.3	100.0
4.7	0.6	0.3	0.7	2.3	100.0
—1.8—		7.1	1.9	0.3	100.0
—0.8—		—5.4—		-	100.0
—1.7—		0.9	1.0	-	100.0
—1.7—				-	100.0
—3.6—		0.2	0.2	1.5	100.0
-	-	2.1	-	11.2	100.0
—4.1—		6.2	1.5	-	100.0
-	-	0.5	0.7	23.2	100.0
-	4.7	1.1	4.0	7.2	100.0

Table 145.   DIRECTION OF TOURISM
PERCENTAGE BREAKDOWN – REGIONS

Western Europe

TO %	FROM Australia	Belgium	Canada	France	Italy	Japan	Nether-lands	New Zealand
Austria	0.8	3.0	0.4	3.6	2.6	0.7	8.4	-
Belgium	-	-	1.0	11.9	4.1	1.7	11.7	-
Cyprus	1.3	0.3[2]	0.7	1.7	0.7	-	0.7	-
Denmark	————			2.0	1.6	2.0	2.9	-
Finland	1.2[1]	1.8[2]	2.4	4.9	1.8	1.8	5.8	
France	0.7[1]	19.6	1.1	-	4.9	1.5	11.3	
W.Germany	1.2[1]	6.0[2]	1.2	6.9	4.4	3.6	17.1	
Greece	2.5	2.4[2]	1.6	6.1	5.0	2.5	2.7	-
Iceland	0.5	1.0	1.4	5.0	1.1	0.5	2.2	0.5
Ireland	-	1.7[2]	1.6	4.7	-	-	2.9	-
Italy	0.7	2.4	0.8	14.2	-	0.8	4.1	0.2
Jersey	-	1.9	-	13.9	-	-	1.6	-
Luxembourg	-	27.6	-	9.8	1.8	-	19.0	-
Malta	0.7	0.9	0.6	2.0	4.4	0.1	1.4	0.1
Netherlands	1.9	4.6	2.1	8.2	2.9	2.3	-	-
Norway	1.0	1.5[2]	1.9	5.4	1.5	1.9	7.6	-
Portugal	0.3[1]	0.9	0.8	3.5	1.3	0.2	2.5	-
San Marino	-	1.2	-	2.5	84.0	-	0.8	-
Spain	0.2	2.9	0.4	29.1	1.2	0.2	3.7	-
Sweden	-	-	0.9	3.7	2.1	2.1	5.5	-
Switzerland	1.5[1]	4.5	1.2	9.0	5.8	4.0	5.2	-
Turkey	0.6	1.4	1.4	7.9	5.3	0.5	1.6	-
UK	3.3	5.0[2]	3.8	11.0	3.3	1.1	7.8	0.7

Source: WTO/OECD/National Offices.

(1) Including New Zealand
(2) Including Luxembourg
(3) Including Portugal

Scandinavia	Spain	Switzerland	U.K.	U.S.A.	West Germany	Others/ Unknown	Total
4.2	0.7	3.6	3.5	4.1	57.8	6.6	100.0
3.2	2.2	1.6	18.8	11.5	15.7	1.6	100.0
7.1	-	1.3	35.7	2.7	6.7	41.1	100.0
30.9	-	-	6.9	9.0	32.4	12.3	100.0
-	1.5	4.3	9.1	12.2	30.1	23.1	100.0
1.5	3.2	7.3	11.4	3.9	25.3	8.3	100.0
11.2	1.6	5.1	9.5	13.5	-	18.7	100.0
10.4	1.0	2.7	10.7	11.5	10.6	30.3	100.0
27.3	0.7	4.5	8.8	29.3	12.6	4.6	100.0
			61.4	15.5	5.1	7.1	100.0
3.2	1.0	17.5	4.1	3.6	22.2	25.2	100.0
-	-	-	78.2	-	1.3	3.1	100.0
0.9	-	2.3	5.0	9.8	14.4	9.4	100.0
3.5	0.1	0.9	70.3	1.4	3.7	9.9	100.0
6.9	2.4[3]	2.8	16.4	11.2	22.9	15.4	100.0
2.9	1.0	1.5	27.6	18.2	20.9	7.1	100.0
2.1	66.5	0.7	7.6	2.9	5.4	5.3	100.0
-	-	1.1	0.4	-	6.9	3.1	100.0
4.0	-	1.6	9.3	2.4	12.6	32.4	100.0
34.4	-	2.3	9.0	11.3	17.5	11.2	100.0
2.8	2.3	-	6.1	10.9	30.7	16.0	100.0
2.5	2.1	2.0	4.6	10.6	13.0	46.5	100.0
8.0	2.5	2.4	-	13.8	12.4	24.9	100.0

Table 146.   **DIRECTION OF TOURISM 1979**
PERCENTAGE BREAKDOWN — REGIONS

Eastern Europe

TO %	FROM West Europe	East Europe	North & Central America	South America
Bulgaria	43.0	51.7	0.2	-
Czechoslovakia	20.8	76.5	———————	
E. Germany	17.3	54.1	———————	———————
Hungary	15.8	82.5	0.7	———————
Poland	8.0	88.8	0.8	-
Romania	11.4	85.1	0.6	0.2
USSR	30.9	57.8	2.9	-
Yugoslavia	80.2	13.3	3.5	———————

Source   WTO/OECD/National Offices.

Middle East & North Africa	Africa	Far East	Oceania	Others/Unknown	Total
1.7	-	-	-	3.4	100.0
2.7				-	100.0
28.6				-	100.0
1.0				-	100.0
0.2	-	0.2	0.1	1.9	100.0
0.7	0.5	1.4		0.1	100.0
-	-	3.1	-	5.3	100.0
3.0				-	100.0

Table 147.　　　　**DIRECTION OF TOURISM 1979**
　　　　PERCENTAGE BREAKDOWN — BY MAJOR COUNTRIES

Eastern Europe

TO %	FROM Australia	Belgium	Canada	France	Italy	Japan	Nether-lands
Bulgaria	-	0.2	-	1.1	0.5	-	0.3
Czechoslovakia	-	-	-	0.7	1.2	-	0.4
Hungary	-	-	0.2	0.4	0.6	-	0.3
Poland	0.1	0.2	0.1	0.9	0.5	0.1	0.3
Romania	-	0.2	0.5	0.9	0.7	0.1	0.3
USSR	-	0.3	0.3	1.8	1.1	1.0	0.3
Yugoslavia	-	1.5	0.5	6.2	9.8	0.2	5.1

Source: WTO/OECD/National Offices.

New Zealand	Scandinavia	Spain	Switzer-land	U.K.	U.S.A.	West Germany	Others/ Unknown	Total
-	0.2	-	0.1	0.9	0.3	3.0	93.4	100.0
-	1.0	-	0.4	0.4	-	10.3	85.6	100.0
-	0.4	-	0.3	0.2	0.6	4.6	92.4	100.0
-	1.8	0.1	0.1	-	0.7	3.3	91.8	100.0
-	1.0	0.4	0.2	1.1	0.1	4.1	90.4	100.0
-	23.0	-	0.3	1.0	2.1	2.6	66.2	100.0
-	2.6	-	2.4	5.7	3.0	31.0	32.0	100.0

Table 148.
DIRECTION OF TOURISM 1979
PERCENTAGE BREAKDOWN – REGIONS

North & Central America

TO %	West Europe	East Europe	North & Central America	South America
Antigua	22.0	-	———————78.0———————	
Aruba	3.2	-	69.2	27.6
Bahamas	9.1	-	87.3	-
Barbados	21.2	-	72.5	3.8
Belize	11.3	-	37.1	———————
Bermuda	4.8	-	93.9	———————
Bonaire	7.1	-	78.6	7.2
British Virgin Isles	4.4	-	94.5	———————
Canada	8.7	0.3	86.8	0.9
Cayman Isles	4.0	-	95.0	-
Costa Rica	7.9	-	77.9	12.4
Dominican Rep.	8.4	-	81.5	8.7
Grenada	34.4	-	62.5	-
Guadeloupe	60.5	-	38.1	0.7
Guatemala	14.3	-	55.1	28.2
Haiti	21.4	-	75.9	-
Jamaica	12.4	-	86.4	0.5
Martinique	55.3	-	———————44.7———————	
Mexico	5.3	-	———————93.5———————	
Montserrat	7.2	-	85.7	-
Panama	5.2	-	53.4	38.1
Puerto Rico	-	-	76.2	-
St. Kitts	4.0	-	92.0	-
St. Vincent	8.6	-	60.0	1.4
Trinidad & Tobago	14.7	-	63.7	20.0
USA	12.2	0.6	73.7	4.2

Source: WTO/OECD/National Offices.

Middle East & North Africa	Africa	Far East	Oceania	Others/Unknown	Total
-	-	-	-	-	100.0
-	-	-	-	-	100.0
	3.6			-	100.0
	2.5			-	100.0
	51.6			-	100.0
	1.3			-	100.0
-	-	-	-	7.1	100.0
	1.1			-	100.0
0.4	0.3	2.6		-	100.0
-	-	-	-	1.0	100.0
-	-	1.5		0.3	100.0
-	-	-	-	1.4	100.0
	3.1			-	100.0
	0.7			-	100.0
-	-	1.6		0.8	100.0
-	-	-	-	2.7	100.0
-	0.2	-	-	0.5	100.0
-	-	-	-	-	100.0
-	-	-	-	1.2	100.0
-	-	-	-	7.1	100.0
-	-	1.0	-	2.3	100.0
-	-	-	-	23.8	100.0
-	-	-	-	4.0	100.0
-	-	-	-	30.0	100.0
-	-	-	-	1.6	100.0
0.3	-	8.2		0.8	100.0

Table 149. DIRECTION OF TOURISM 1979
PERCENTAGE BREAKDOWN — MAJOR COUNTRIES

North & Central America

TO %	FROM Australia	Belgium	Canada	France	Italy	Japan	Nether- lands
Antigua	-	-	10.0	-	-	-	-
Aruba	-	-	3.8	-	-	-	2.2
Bahamas	-	-	11.9	-	-	-	-
Barbados	-	0.3	28.8	0.6	0.3	-	0.6
Belize	-	-	4.8	-	-	-	-
Bermuda	-	-	7.0	-	-	-	-
Bonaire	-	-	5.9	-	-	-	11.7
British Virgin Isles	-	-	3.3	-	-	-	-
Canada	0.5	0.2	-	0.9	0.4	1.0	0.7
Cayman Isles	-	-	5.9	-	-	-	-
Costa Rica	-	-	1.7	-	0.9	-	1.2
Dominican Rep.	-	-	1.7	1.1	1.0	-	-
Grenada	-	-	9.4	-	-	-	-
Guadeloupe	-	0.7	10.2	43.5	2.0	-	-
Guatemala	-	0.4	1.8	2.8	2.0	1.0	0.8
Haiti	-	0.9	12.5	8.9	0.9	-	1.8
Jamaica	0.1	0.2	17.3	0.2	0.2	-	0.2
Martinique	-	-	6.9	37.1	-	-	-
Meixco	-	-	4.4	-	-	-	-
Montserrat	-	-	14.3	-	-	-	-
Panama	-	-	1.3	0.5	0.8	1.0	0.3
Puerto Rico	-	-	4.5	0.2	0.2	-	-
St. Kitts	-	-	4.0	-	-	-	-
St. Vincent	-	-	4.3	1.4	-	-	-
Trinidad & Tobago	-	-	13.2	-	-	-	-
USA	0.9	0.3	60.3	1.3	0.8	4.5	0.7

Source: WTO/OECD/National Offices.

New Zealand	Scandinavia	Spain	Switzerland	U.K.	U.S.A.	West Germany	Others/ Unknown	Total
-	-	-	-	-	44.0	-	24.0	100.0
-	-	-	-	-	64.3	-	29.7	100.0
-	-	-	-	-	75.5	-	12.6	100.0
-	1.3	-	1.0	11.4	26.9	4.7	24.1	100.0
-	-	-	-	-	32.3	-	62.9	100.0
-	-	-	-	3.7	86.7	-	2.6	100.0
-	-	-	-	-	41.2	-	41.2	100.0
-	-	-	-	1.1	68.1	-	27.5	100.0
0.1	0.4	0.1	0.3	3.8	86.1	1.5	4.0	100.0
-	-	-	-	2.0	76.2	1.0	14.9	100.0
-	-	1.5	-	-	21.5	1.4	71.8	100.0
-	-	2.1	-	0.7	72.8	1.1	19.5	100.0
-	-	-	-	-	28.1	-	62.5	100.0
-	-	-	10.2	0.7	27.2	2.1	3.4	100.0
-	-	1.4	1.2	1.2	21.2	3.5	62.7	100.0
-	0.9	0.4	2.7	1.8	50.9	3.6	14.7	100.0
-	0.5	-	1.9	2.1	65.6	6.1	5.6	100.0
-	-	-	-	-	28.3	-	27.7	100.0
-	-	-	-	-	83.0	-	12.6	100.0
-	-	-	-	-	42.8	-	42.9	100.0
-	-	1.3	0.5	17.4	0.8	1.0	75.1	100.0
-	-	0.5	-	0.2	79.1	-	15.3	100.0
-	-	-	-	4.0	52.0	-	40.0	100.0
-	1.4	-	-	4.3	14.3	1.4	72.9	100.0
-	-	-	-	8.9	29.5	-	48.4	100.0
0.4	1.1	0.3	0.6	3.8	-	2.5	22.5	100.0

Table 150. DIRECTION OF TOURISM 1979
PERCENTAGE BREAKDOWN — REGIONS

South America

TO %	FROM West Europe	East Europe	North & Central America	South America
Bolivia	——————43.9——————		19.2	32.5
Brazil	21.6	-	12.4	63.0
Colombia	——————6.4——————		17.0	75.5
Chile	10.2	-	10.2	73.7
Ecuador	18.8	-	26.3	36.6
El Salvador	4.3	-	89.6	4.4
Paraguay	0.7	-	1.0	79.8
Peru	32.1	-	26.2	35.1
Suriname	66.6	-	12.5	16.7
Uruguay	-	-	——————95.2——————	
Venezuela	——————23.6——————		55.1	19.9

Source: WTO/OECD/National Offices.

Middle East & North Africa	Africa	Far East	Oceania	Others/Unknown	Total
4.4				-	100.0
3.0				-	100.0
-	-	-	-	1.1	100.0
-	-	2.4		3.5	100.0
-	-	1.2	-	7.1	100.0
-	-	1.3		0.4	100.0
N/R	N/R	1.6	N/R	16.9	100.0
4.8				1.8	100.0
4.2				-	100.0
-	-	-	-	4.8	100.0
N/R	N/R	0.6	N/R	0.8	100.0

Table 151. **DIRECTION OF TOURISM 1979**
PERCENTAGE BREAKDOWN — MAJOR COUNTRIES

South America

TO %	FROM Australia	Belgium	Canada	France	Italy	Japan	Netherlands
Bolivia	-	-	3.0	10.8	3.4	2.5	-
Brazil	0.4	0.4	1.0	3.0	3.2	1.9	0.7
Colombia	-	-	0.8	0.9	0.8	-	-
Chile	1.0	-	1.0	1.8	1.4	1.4	-
Ecuador	-	-	2.1	2.9	2.5	1.3	0.8
El Salvador	-	-	0.9				
Paraguay					-	1.7	-
Peru	0.6	0.9	2.4	6.5	3.6	3.3	1.5
Suriname	-	-	-	2.1	-	-	62.5
Venezuela	-	-	3.1	2.0	3.5	0.6	5.6

Source: WTO/OECD/National Offices.

New Zealand	Scandinavia	Spain	Switzerland	U.K.	U.S.A.	West Germany	Others/ Unknown	Total
-	-	2.0	4.4	3.0	14.8	12.3	43.8	100.0
-	1.0	2.4	1.5	2.1	10.5	4.5	67.4	100.0
-	-	1.0	0.4	0.7	8.5	1.2	85.7	100.0
-	-	1.8	0.7	1.4	9.5	3.2	76.8	100.0
-	-	2.5	2.1	2.1	22.5	5.4	55.8	100.0
—	-	0.4	-	-	12.1	0.4	86.2	100.0
-	-	0.3	-	-	1.0	0.3	96.7	100.0
0.3	0.9	3.3	3.0	3.0	21.1	8.3	41.3	100.0
-	-	-	-	2.1	6.2	-	27.1	100.0
-	-	3.2	0.9	2.9	46.4	2.8	29.0	100.0

Table 152.   DIRECTION OF TOURISM 1979
PERCENTAGE BREAKDOWN – REGIONS

North Africa & Middle East

TO %	FROM West Europe	East Europe	North & Central America	South America	Middle East & North Africa
Algeria	60.5	5.0	4.2	0.4	23.4
Iran	41.7	1.8	13.9	-	12.5
Iraq	11.2	1.7	0.4	-	61.4
Israel	59.2	0.4	29.0	3.1	1.1
Jordan	9.4	-	5.7	0.2	63.2
Lebanon	13.1	0.8	2.5	-	41.8
Libya	38.0	-	4.3	-	41.7
Morocco	60.7	-	7.2	-	1.4
Syria	——8.8——		———1.6———		72.4
Tunisia	77.5	1.0	1.0	-	17.9
Yemen, Rep.	40.5	-	-	-	19.0

Source: WTO/OECD/National Offices.

Africa	Far East	Oceania	Unknown/Others	Total
1.9	————1.9————		2.7	100.0
-	15.9	1.3	12.9	100.0
15.3	3.3	-	6.7	100.0
2.9	1.9	1.6	0.8	100.0
18.2	————3.3————		-	100.0
3.3	1.6	-	36.9	100.0
1.9	————4.3————		9.8	100.0
24.9	-	0.5	5.3	100.0
4.2	————12.2————		0.8	100.0
0.2	-	-	2.4	100.0
26.2	————14.3————		-	100.0

Table 153.   DIRECTION OF TOURISM 1979
PERCENTAGE BREAKDOWN — BY MAJOR COUNTRIES

North Africa & Middle East

TO % FROM	Australia	Belgium	Canada	France	Italy	Japan	Nether-lands	New Zealand
Algeria	-	2.3	1.5	35.6	7.3	-	0.8	-
Iran	1.1	-	1.3	4.7	4.9	3.9	1.5	0.3
Iraq	-	-	-	0.9	0.3	0.8	-	-
Israel	1.4	2.0	2.9	11.7	3.7	0.4	3.8	0.2
Jordan	0.2	0.1	0.4	0.7	0.6	-	0.2	-
Lebanon	-	0.8[1]	-	2.5	1.6	0.8	-	-
Libya	0.6	-	0.6	3.1	17.2	-	-	-
Morocco	0.6	2.4	1.3	22.5	2.2	-	2.0	-
Tunisia	-	3.0	0.2	30.8	5.0	-	3.5	-
Yemen, Rep	-	-	-	7.1	4.8	2.4	2.4	-

Source: WTO/OECD/National Offices.

(1) Including The Netherlands
(2) Including Portugal
(3) Including Austria
(4) Including Canada

Scandinavia	Spain	Switzerland	U.K.	U.S.A.	West Germany	Others/ Unknown	Total
1.1	2.7	2.3	3.1	2.7	4.6	36.0	100.0
1.9	-	1.1	9.7	12.6	8.1	48.9	100.0
-	-	-	0.7	0.4	1.1	95.8	100.0
7.0	0.6	3.1	11.0	25.5	11.4	15.3	100.0
0.3	-	-	1.6	5.3	1.6	89.0	100.0
0.8	-	0.8[3]	2.5	2.5[4]	1.6	86.1	100.0
0.6	0.6[2]	0.6	6.7	3.1	4.3	62.6	100.0
4.5	9.4	1.7	7.5	5.9	7.0	33.0	100.0
3.3	0.7	2.7	7.7	0.8	18.5	23.8	100.0
2.4	-	2.4	7.1	-	7.1	64.3	100.0

Table 154.   DIRECTION OF TOURISM 1979
PERCENTAGE BREAKDOWN — REGIONS

Africa

TO %	FROM West Europe	East Europe	North & Central America	South America
Benin	34.2	2.4	4.9	-
Botswana	4.9	-	1.3	-
Comoros	76.5	-	3.0	-
Congo	58.3	4.1	——4.2——	
Egypt	37.1	2.9	——15.7——	
Ethiopia	17.6	-	5.9	-
Gambia	93.7	-	——————	
Ghana	24.5	-	8.9	-
Ivory Coast	55.8	-	5.0	0.5
Kenya	58.0	-	9.9	-
Madagascar	63.6	-	-	-
Malawi	18.7	-	2.1	-
Mauritius	36.6	-	0.8	-
Niger	68.7	-	6.3	-
Senegal	71.2	1.0	——8.1——	
Seychelles	64.6	-	——5.1——	
Sudan	33.3	3.7	7.4	-
Swaziland	——5.7——		——2.9——	
Tanzania	——42.9——		——11.3——	
Togo	44.8	-	6.0	-
Zaire	61.5	-	7.7	-
Zambia	24.5	-	3.8	1.9

Source: WTO/OECD/National Offices.

Middle East & North Africa	Africa	Far East	Oceania	Others/Unknown	Total
2.4	48.8	-	-	7.3	100.0
-	93.4	——0.4——		-	100.0
2.2	17.8	0.5	-	-	100.0
-	29.2	-	-	4.2	100.0
27.3	10.9	4.8	0.9	0.4	100.0
5.9	29.4	——8.8——		32.4	100.0
——6.3——				-	100.0
2.2	57.8	4.4	-	2.2	100.0
33.2	3.0	1.0	-	1.5	100.0
0.8	21.9	6.8	1.0	1.6	100.0
-	27.3	——9.1——		-	100.0
2.1	75.0	-	-	2.1	100.0
-	53.7	2.4	0.8	5.7	100.0
-	18.8	-	-	6.2	100.0
——18.7——		——0.5——		0.5	100.0
——20.2——		——10.1——		-	100.0
11.1	29.6	7.4	-	7.5	100.0
——85.7——		——1.4——		4.3	100.0
——19.7——		——26.1——		-	100.0
——46.3——		——1.5——		1.4	100.0
——19.2——		——3.9——		7.7	100.0
——66.0——		——3.8——		-	100.0

Table 155.   DIRECTION OF TOURISM 1979
PERCENTAGE BREAKDOWN – MAJOR COUNTRIES

Africa

TO %	FROM Australia	Belgium	Canada	France	Italy	Japan	Netherlands
Benin	-	2.4	2.5	17.1	2.4	-	2.4
Botswana	0.4[1]	Not available					
Comoros	-	-	-	100	-	-	-
Congo	-	-	-	37.5	4.2	-	4.2
Egypt	0.9	-	1.1	7.3	5.1	1.7	-
Ethiopia	-	-	-	5.9	2.9	-	-
Gambia	-	-	-	-	-	-	-
Ghana	-	-	2.2	-	2.2	2.2	2.2
Ivory Coast	-	2.0	1.0	39.7	3.5	1.0	1.0
Kenya	1.0[1]	1.0	1.3	4.7	5.5	1.3	1.6
Madagascar	-	-	-	27.3	18.2	-	-
Malawi	-	-	See USA	-	-	-	-
Mauritius	-	0.8	-	21.1	3.3	-	-
Niger	-	-	6.3	31.2	6.2	-	-
Senegal	-	-	1.5	38.4	4.0		
Seychelles	-	1.3[2]	-	19.0	10.1	2.5	-
Sudan	1.0	-	-	3.2	6.4	1.1	1.1
Togo	-	-	1.5	20.9	1.5	-	-
Zaire	-	34.6	-	11.5	3.8	-	-
Zambia	-	-	-	1.9	1.9	-	-

Source: WTO/OECD/National Offices.

(1) Including New Zealand
(2) Including Luxembourg
(3) Including Portugal
(4) Including Eire
(5) Including Canada

184

New Zealand	Scandinavia	Spain	Switzerland	U.K.	U.S.A.	West Germany	Others/ Unknown	Total
-	2.4	-	2.4	2.5	2.5	4.9	58.5	100.0
Not available				2.7[4]	0.9	-	96.0	100.0
-	-	-	-	-	-	-	-	100.0
-	-	-	-	-	-	4.1	50.0	100.0
-	1.9	1.2	1.4	6.3	13.2	7.4	52.5	100.0
-	-	-	-	5.9	5.9	2.9	76.5	100.0
-	80.0	-	6.7	-	-	13.3	-	100.0
-	2.2	-	2.2	11.1	6.7	4.5	64.5	100.0
-	1.0	1.0	1.5	3.0	3.5	2.5	39.3	100.0
-	2.6	-	7.1	14.6	8.6	17.5	33.2	100.0
-	-	-	-	-	-	9.1	45.4	100.0
Not available				10.4	2.1[5]	-	87.5	100.0
0.8	-	-	0.8	6.5	0.8	4.9	61.0	100.0
-	-	-	-	-	-	18.8	37.5	100.0
———	1.0	2.0[3]	5.1	2.0	5.6	12.1	28.3	100.0
-	1.3	1.3[3]	5.1	16.4	-	6.3	36.7	100.0
-	0.3	-	0.8	15.6	6.6	4.9	59.0	100.0
-	1.5	-	4.5	3.0	4.5	7.4	55.2	100.0
-	-	-	3.8	3.9	3.9	3.9	34.6	100.0
-	Not available			11.3	3.8	1.9	79.2	100.0

Source: WTO/OECD/National Offices.

Table 156.   DIRECTION OF TOURISM 1979
PERCENTAGE BREAKDOWN – REGIONS

Far East

TO %	FROM		North & Central	
	West Europe	East Europe	America	South America
Afghanistan	——————32.4——————		5.4	-
Bangladesh	19.3	1.7	8.8	-
Brunei	6.0	-	1.5	-
Guam	-	-	——————13.6——————	
Hong Kong	13.7	0.1	16.2	1.0
India	37.0	1.8	14.1	-
Indonesia	34.1	0.2	——————11.8——————	
Japan	18.7	1.1	31.0	2.6
Korea (S)	3.8	-	12.5	-
Macau	21.7	-	7.3	0.5
Malaysia	11.8	0.4	6.2	-
Nepal	42.6	-	13.6	-
Pakistan	32.3	0.6	6.3	-
Philippines	18.3	-	15.8	0.1
Samoa	10	-	25	-
Singapore	15.3	-	6.1	-
Sri Lanka	67.2	2.0	5.6	-
Taiwan	4.7	-	10.8	0.7
Thailand	31.4	-	8.5	-

Source: WTO/OECD/National Offices.

Middle East & North Africa	Africa	Far East	Oceania	Others/Unknown	Total
2.7	-	54.1	5.4	-	100.0
1.7	-	63.2	1.8	3.5	100.0
-	-	90.2	1.2	1.1	100.0
-	-	———72.4———		14.0	100.0
1.2	0.9	58.7	7.8	0.4	100.0
7.8	1.6	19.6	3.8	14.3	100.0
0.6	0.2	38.9	13.4	0.8	100.0
0.3	0.8	42.6	2.7	0.2	100.0
-	-	———71.0———		12.7	100.0
0.8	0.3	63.5	4.5	1.4	100.0
-	-	71.3	7.5	2.8	100.0
-	-	31.5	5.5	6.8	100.0
4.1	0.3	45.4	1.6	9.4	100.0
-	-	57.2	6.4	2.2	100.0
-	-	———60———		5	100.0
-	-	61.4	11.9	5.3	100.0
-	-	22.4	2.8	-	100.0
———0.5———		82.0	1.3	-	100.0
2.8	-	50.9	4.5	1.9	100.0

Table 157. **DIRECTION OF TOURISM 1979**
PERCENTAGE BREAKDOWN — MAJOR COUNTRIES

Far East

TO % FROM	Australia	Belgium	Canada	France	Italy	Japan	Netherlands
Afghanistan	2.7	-	-	2.7	2.7	2.7	-
Bangladesh	1.8	-	1.8	1.8	-	5.2	1.7
Brunei	0.7	-	0.4	-	-	82.3	0.8
Guam	-	-	-	-	-	72.3	-
Hong Kong	6.3	0.3	2.3	1.8	1.2	23.0	0.6
India	3.1	1.1	3.1	6.9	3.5	3.9	1.4
Indonesia	12.1	0.6	1.6	5.4	3.0	10.6	7.2
Japan	2.2	0.4	3.1	2.0	1.0	-	0.9
Korea (S)	0.5	0.1	0.5	0.5	0.2	61.3	0.2
Macau	4.0	0.2	1.2	1.2	0.5	35.1	0.3
Malaysia	7.5	-	1.2	-	-	7.3	-
Nepal	4.9	1.2	1.9	11.1	3.7	7.4	1.9
Pakistan	1.3	0.3	1.6	1.9	0.9	1.9	0.3
Philippines	6.0	0.2	1.2	1.0	1.0	26.9	0.6
Samoa	10.0	-	5.0	-	-	-	-
Singapore	9.2	0.4[1]	0.8	1.9	1.0	11.1	1.9
Sri Lanka	2.4	1.2	1.2	12.4	4.0	4.0	2.0
Taiwan	1.2	-	1.0	0.5	0.3	63.4	0.4
Thailand	3.9	0.9	1.1	4.6	3.0	12.6	1.5

Source: WTO/OECD/National Offices.

(1) Including Luxembourg
(2)   "   Canada

New Zealand	Scandi-navia	Spain	Switzer-land	U.K.	U.S.A.	West Germany	Others/Unknown	Total
-	-	-	-	5.4	2.7	5.4	75.7	100.0
-	3.5	-	-	8.8	7.0	3.5	64.9	100.0
0.4	0.4	-	-	4.1	1.1	0.4	9.4	100.0
-	-	-	-	-	13.7[2]	-	14.0	100.0
1.3	0.7	0.4	0.8	4.3	13.7	2.6	40.7	100.0
0.7	1.6	-	1.6	13.2	10.7	6.7	42.5	100.0
1.2	1.4	0.8	1.8	7.0	9.4	6.2	31.7	100.0
0.4	1.9	0.5	0.8	6.5	27.1	3.4	49.8	100.0
-	0.3	-	0.2	1.1	12.0	1.0	22.1	100.0
0.5	0.2	0.3	0.3	17.7	5.9	1.2	31.4	100.0
See Aust.	-	-	-	6.1	5.0	-	72.9	100.0
1.2	2.5	3.1	1.9	6.8	11.7	8.0	32.7	100.0
0.3	0.6	0.3	0.3	24.5	4.7	2.8	58.3	100.0
2.7	0.8	0.6	0.8	10.0	14.5	2.4	31.3	100.0
25.0	-	-	-	10.0	20.0	-	30.0	100.0
2.7	1.2	-	0.8	5.2	5.3	2.9	55.6	100.0
0.4	8.8	1.2	4.4	7.6	4.4	20.4	25.6	100.0
0.1	-	0.1	0.3	1.0	9.7	1.3	20.7	100.0
0.6	3.3	1.2	1.6	8.0	7.2	6.2	44.3	100.0

Table 158. DIRECTION OF TOURISM 1979
PERCENTAGE BREAKDOWN — REGIONS

Oceania

TO %	FROM West Europe	East Europe	North & Central America	South America
Australia	26.9	0.4	15.0	0.8
Cook Islands	5.9	-	11.8	-
Fiji	6.4	-	19.6	-
French Polynesia	25.7	-	51.5	5.0
Hawaii	2.0	-	66.3	0.6
New Caledonia	27.3	-	3.6	-
New Hebrides	42.9	-	2.9	-
New Zealand	11.8	0.2	17.3	0.5
Papua New Guinea	12.1	-	9.1	-
Tonga	8.3	-	16.7	-
Western Samoa	9.1	-	31.8	-

Source : WTO/OECD/National Offices.

190

Middle East & North Africa	Africa	Far East	Oceania	Others/Unknown	Total
-	1.6	14.6	40.1	0.6	100.0
-	-	-	70.6	11.7	100.0
-	-	2.6	68.8	2.6	100.0
-	-	5.9	10.9	1.0	100.0
-	0.1	20.0	11.0	-	100.0
-	-	21.8	38.2	9.1	100.0
			51.4	2.8	100.0
-	0.7	6.7	54.2	8.6	100.0
-	-	15.2	63.6	-	100.0
-	-	-	66.7	8.3	100.0
-	-	——54.5——		4.6	100.0

Table 159.   DIRECTION OF TOURISM 1979
PERCENTAGE BREAKDOWN — MAJOR COUNTRIES

Oceania

TO %	FROM Australia	Belgium	Canada	France	Italy	Japan	Nether-lands
Australia	-	0.1	2.9	0.9	1.4	5.3	2.0
Cook Islands	5.9	-	-	-	-	-	-
Fiji	38.6	-	5.3	-	-	2.6	-
French Polynesia	7.9	-	5.9	13.9	4.0	5.0	-
Hawaii	-	-	7.5	-	-	20.0	-
New Caledonia	29.1	-	-	16.4	-	21.8	-
New Hebrides	31.4	-	0.7	34.3	0.4	8.6	-
New Zealand	50.9	-	3.3	1.4	-	3.7	-
Papua New Guinea	54.5	-	-	-	-	6.1	-
Solomon Islands	35.0	-	-	-	-	-	-
Tonga	16.7	-	-	-	-	-	-
Western Samoa	23.9	-	5.0	-	-	-	-

Source :WTO/OECD/National Offices.

New Zealand	Scandi-navia	Spain	Switzer-land	U.K.	U.S.A.	West Germany	Others/Unknown	Total
34.6	-	0.1	0.9	14.8	12.1	-	24.9	100.0
47.0	-	-	-	5.9	11.8	-	29.4	100.0
23.3	-	-	-	2.7	14.3	-	13.2	100.0
4.0	-	-	1.0	2.0	45.4	4.0	6.9	100.0
-	-	-	-	-	58.8	-	13.7	100.0
9.1	Not available						23.6	100.0
8.6	-	-	-	8.6	2.9	0.8	3.7	100.0
-	0.9	0.2	-	7.4	13.9	-	18.3	100.0
6.1	-	-	-	3.0	9.1	3.0	18.2	100.0
-	-	-	-	-	11.3	-	53.7	100.0
33.3	-	-	-	-	16.7	8.3	25.0	100.0
17.3	-	-	-	1.2	24.9	-	27.7	100.0

CHAPTER SEVEN
INCENTIVES OF TRAVEL

In this chapter, we shall be looking at the reasons why people travel to overseas countries, and in doing so, we must return to the vexed question of definition. Often, the word "tourist" is used to mean a person travelling to another country for a holiday, or some leisure-orientated activity. But as the travel industry knows only too well, tourism also incorporates the lucrative business market, and various other reasons and purposes for travel. In this section, we shall try to establish how the world travel market is split between these various travel incentives.

Returning to the definition of tourism used by the World Tourism Organisation, the following would be legitimate purposes of visit for a tourist:-

1. Travel for a holiday, leisure, recreation, sport.
2. Business travel.
3. Travel to conferences.
4. Visits to friends and relatives.
5. Visits, of short duration, by government officials, e.g. "missions".
6. Health.
7. Study — again of short duration.
8. Religion.

Various other reasons for visiting countries are excluded from the standard definition, and from the scope of this study. These are reasons which involve very temporary stays, such as a 24 hour stopover in transit, or an overnight stay by a cruise passenger. Others would be excluded because they would be longer in duration, such as a lengthy study period, or a one year stay by a businessman or politician. These are generally termed "visitors", and I have tried to exclude these categories from all my figures. This is particularly difficult in considering purpose of visit, however, because many reported figures do refer to all visits, not just tourist arrivals.

We can see now why figures on tourist arrivals are not compatible with tourist arrivals at registered accommodation, and it is not only because all accommodation is not registered. We can see that some of the above categories, which would all be termed "tourist arrivals", would not stay in paid accommodation i.e. people visiting friends and relatives, and some would probably not stay in standard tourist accommodation — i.e. students, or possibly visitors for health or religious reasons. So definitions have to be consistent if figures are to mean anything and reasons for visits are very important to the travel industry.

Some work has been done on the types of tourists using the larger hotels, by Horwath & Horwath International. Their figures, which are based on sample surveys, show the types of tourist visitors using hotels in the main world regions, and although they include domestic and international tourists, they do provide a useful indication of hotel usership.

Their total figures for the world show that the number of foreign visitors staying in hotels is on the decrease as a proportion of the whole, down from two-thirds in 1978 to just over half in 1980. But we are more concerned here with their breakdown of types of visitors, and their findings are insteresting; the largest proportion of persons staying in hotels — with over two-fifths of the total — are businessmen, while business-orientated visitors such as conference participants and government officials account for a further 17%. So holidaymakers (which they call tourists) account for under one-third of the world's hotel consumption, and a declining proportion since 1978.

Looking regionally at the types of visitors using hotels, we discover a not unexpected pattern of demand. The stronger holiday markets, such as The Caribbean and Mexico, have a higher incidence of holiday travellers than the less attractive destinations. But in the U.S.A., Canada and Europe, a low proportion of hotel users are on holiday. Most are on business.

Table 160.   Composition of World Hotel Consumption 1978-1980

	1978	1979	1980
Foreign visitors	62.6%	57.2%	53.9%
Domestic visitors	37.4%	42.8%	46.1%
Total	100.0%	100.0%	100.0%
Government officials	5.5%	6.2%	6.1%
Businessmen	40.2%	40.5%	42.0%
Holidaymakers	33.5%	30.9%	30.7%
Conference participants	10.7%	12.8%	10.8%
Other	10.1%	9.6%	10.4%
Total	100.0%	100.0%	100.0%
% booked in advance through travel agents or tour operators	24.1%	22.6%	22.2%

Source: Horwath & Horwath International, based on a worldwide sample of hotels.

Table 161. Hotel Composition by Region 1980

	Tourists	Businessmen	Attending Conferences	Other*
World	31%	42%	11%	16%
Africa	46%	25%	7%	22%
Asia	46%	28%	7%	17%
Oceania	19%	48%	9%	24%
Caribbean	76%	13%	7%	4%
Central America	23%	54%	2%	21%
Europe	24%	49%	13%	14%
Far East	38%	38%	5%	19%
Middle East	18%	42%	7%	33%
Canada	25%	40%	16%	24%
U.S.A.	32%	40%	18%	10%
Mexico	47%	33%	12%	8%
South America	13%	70%	8%	9%

Source: Horwath & Horwath International
Note: Rounded figures   * Including Government officials

We can see, therefore, that the business travel market is extremely important to the hotel industry, but what proportion of total tourist arrivals are for business purposes?

The World Tourism Organisation does collect figures on purpose of visit, and some countries publish similar figures either on reasons for their population travelling overseas, or reasons why people visit their country. I am, however, dubious about the usefulness of the tourist intake breakdowns, because of the different data bases used. Instead, I have taken a cross-section of countries where the figures seemed to correlate in order to produce an estimated analysis of world travel by purpose of visit. The figures have been rounded because they are only rough approximations, but my conclusion is that the total world consumption of tourists is as follows:-

Holidays and recreation	65%
Business	15%
Visits to friends and relatives	15%
Other, including study, health, religious, missions etc.	5%
Total	100%

Table 162. Tourist Visits by Region and Purpose of Visit 1980

	Holiday	Business	Other	Total
North West Europe	45%	20%	35%	100%
Southern Europe	80%	10%	10%	100%
Total West Europe	55%	18%	27%	100%
Eastern Europe	70%	8%	22%	100%
The Caribbean	90%	5%	5%	100%
U.S.A.	82%	10%	8%	100%
Canada	60%	12%	28%	100%
Mexico	70%	10%	20%	100%
Total North & Central America	80%	10%	10%	100%
Brazil	50%	45%	5%	100%
Other South America	75%	10%	15%	100%
Total South America	70%	15%	10%	100%
North Africa	85%	8%	7%	100%
Middle East	25%	50%	25%	100%
Total	50%	33%	17%	100%
Africa	60%	25%	15%	100%
Far East	70%	18%	12%	100%
Australia	40%	16%	44%	100%
Pacific Islands	80%	5%	15%	100%
Total Oceanic	70%	8%	22%	100%
Total World	65%	15%	20%	100%

Source: Own Estimates

198

Looking first at **Western Europe**, there is here a strong contrast between the holiday-orientated Mediterranean countries, and the North West, which has a larger business market. But the business market is small in **Eastern Europe**, where only 8% of tourists visit for business reasons.

The Caribbean is heavily veered towards holiday travel, and here 90% of tourists are on holiday. This is less for the U.S.A., and especially Canada, bringing the average for **North and Central America** down to 80% holiday, and 10% business.

Most of the countries in **South America** focus on holiday travel, but travel to Brazil is heavily business-orientated, and this brings down the average to 70% holiday, and 15% business.

The **North Africa and Middle East** region throws up considerable contrasts. The main holiday markets of the North African coast make tourist intake here veer heavily towards holiday travel, but the Middle East market is around 50% business — the highest proportion for business in all the regions. **Africa**, too, has a fairly high business market, which decreases through the **Far East** to small proportions in **Oceania**.

To conclude this chapter, we shall look at the reasons why residents from some of the main travelling nations travel to other countries. The countries surveyed are the U.S.A., Canada, Britain and Australia.

TRAVEL FROM U.S.A. BY PURPOSE OF VISIT

Figures on travel from the U.S.A. refer to household trips in 1977. They show that trips for all types of holiday reasons (including sightseeing, outdoor recreation entertainment and shopping) accounted for around one half of the total number of overseas trips, while business trips accounted for 15%.

Business travel from the U.S. was most important when the destinations were developing countries; it accounted for 46% of trips to Africa, 30% to Asia and South America. Visits to friends and relatives were important in trips to Europe, and Asia along with Mexico and Canada as one would expect. The proportion of total trips devoted to travel stayed fairly steady at 50% when all the holiday categories were taken into account, although there were considerable fluctuations within these categories.

Table 163.   Travel by U.S. Households in Overseas Countries by Purpose of Visit 1977

	1.	2.	3.	4.	5.	6.	7.	8.	9.	10. 100% =
Canada	19.9	13.7	2.5	19.0	11.5	23.6	5.1	0.5	4.2	3,830
Mexico	29.4	8.4	1.0	15.3	12.0	14.8	9.9	4.5	4.8	1,991
Other North America	5.6	8.2	0.9	12.9	49.1	14.2	1.7	-	7.3	232
Central and South America	17.7	29.6	1.0	13.8	4.9	22.8	5.3	-	5.1	412
Caribbean	13.2	16.3	1.6	12.7	25.6	15.4	4.3	-	10.8	1,401
Western Europe	21.3	18.4	1.3	2.3	8.9	35.5	4.4	1.0	6.7	1,682
Eastern Europe	30.4	9.5	3.2	4.4	-	42.4	4.4	-	5.1	158
Oceania	7.1	20.0	-	12.5	19.6	41.1	-	-	-	56
Africa	13.1	45.9	4.1	3.3	3.3	25.4	-	-	4.9	122
Asia	27.1	30.7	-	-	1.3	25.0	5.8	-	10.0	479
Total	21.0	15.5	1.7	13.1	13.0	22.9	5.7	1.2	6.0	10,363

Source: National Travel Survey, Bureau of the Census, Washington DC.

Key: 1. Visit friends and relatives
        2. Business
        3. Convention
        4. Outdoor recreation
        5. Entertainment
        6. Sightseeing
        7. Family affairs, personal, medical
        8. Shopping
        9. Other
        10. Total

TRAVEL FROM CANADA BY PURPOSE OF VISIT

The figures on Canadian overseas travel refer to 1973. They show that overall, the business sector is quite small, at 10% of the total, with holidays and recreation close to my estimated world average of 65%. The proportion visiting friends is high, particularly among visits to the United Kingdom, and Europe in general. The figures exclude visits to the United States.

The largest business markets for Canadians are Asia (28% of trips) and South America (35% of trips).

Table 164. Purpose of Trip, by Area of Destination, Canadian Residents Returning from Countries Other than the United States 1973

(per cent)	Business	Holiday and Recreation	Visiting Friends or Relatives	Other	Total 100% =
United Kingdom only	8.2	44.0	46.9	0.9	269,100
United Kingdom and other Europe	15.0	66.0	17.8	1.2	181,400
Other Europe	12.7	48.5	36.8	2.0	349,400
Europe and one other area of destination	16.0	70.5	12.0	1.5	27,500
Africa	11.6	79.1	7.9	1.4	21,600
Asia	27.6	40.1	31.8	0.5	21,700
Central America, Bermuda and Caribbean	7.0	84.1	8.8	0.1	270,300
South America	35.2	46.3	17.6	0.9	10,800
Hawaii	5.4	91.5	3.1	-	68,000
Other areas	6.1	86.3	7.3	0.3	98,700
Cruises	1.1	98.9	-	-	37,400
Combined destinations	23.3	53.5	23.2	-	4,300
Total	10.3	64.1	24.6	1.0	1,360,200

Source: Travel between Canada and Other Countries / Statistics Canada

TRAVEL FROM THE UNITED KINGDOM BY PURPOSE OF VISIT

Figures on overseas travel by U.K. residents refer to 1979, showing that overall, almost two-thirds of overseas trips are for holiday reasons — again close to the estimated world average. The business proportion is 16%, close to the U.S. percentage, and the world average.

The regional analysis shows some marked contrasts. The largest holiday market is Europe excluding the EEC countries, where 85% of visits were for holidays. Business travel accounted for a third of trips to Africa, and a quarter of trips to the States. Visits to friends and relatives were high to the Commonwealth countries — over 50% to Canada, over 60% to Australia.

Table 165. Overseas Travel by U.K. Residents in 1979: Purpose of Visit

	Holiday				Business		Friends/ Relatives		Misc.		Total	
	Inclusive		Independent									
	'000s	%	'000s	%	'000s	%	'000s	%	'000s	%	'000s	%
USA	75	9.3	318	39.4	197	24.4	179	22.2	39	4.8	808	100.0
Canada	4	1.4	93	33.5	19	6.8	149	53.6	12	4.3	278	100.0
Western Europe (EEC)	1,299	16.3	3,044	38.1	1,672	20.9	1,232	15.4	738	9.2	7,985	100.0
Other Western Europe	3,293	66.2	985	19.8	365	7.3	246	4.9	86	1.7	4,974	100.0
Middle East	21	10.6	44	22.2	65	32.8	50	25.3	18	9.1	198	100.0
North Africa	112	54.4	25	12.1	47	22.8	16	7.8	6	2.9	206	100.0
South Africa	2	3.5	24	42.1	11	19.3	18	31.6	2	3.5	57	100.0
Other Africa	12	10.8	36	32.4	31	27.9	30	27.0	2	1.8	111	100.0
Eastern Europe	90	48.6	14	7.6	33	17.8	40	21.6	7	3.8	185	100.0
Australia	-	-	14	18.4	13	17.1	46	60.5	3	3.9	76	100.0
World	5,076	32.8	4,751	30.7	2,542	16.5	2,166	14.0	931	6.0	15,466	100.0

Source: International Passenger Survey, Department of Trade & Industry, London

202

TRAVEL FROM AUSTRALIA BY PURPOSE OF VISIT

Figures for Australia, for 1978, reveal a similar pattern as before; the holiday market share is 60%, the business share about 15%. Visits to friends and relatives account for one-fifth of the total, one-third in Africa and Europe. Business travel is most important in The Americas and Asia.

*   *   *

So, about two-thirds of the world travel market is accounted for by holiday travel, and about 15% by business travel. The rest is mainly travel involving visits to friends and relatives. We can conclude that roughly 80% of the world's travellers are seeking paid accommodation when they travel to overseas countries, the rest staying mainly in private homes. But if the holiday travel sector dominates in terms of total tourist arrivals, the use of the larger hotels is heavily concentrated on the business and conference travel market.

Table 166. Short-Term Movement: Australian Residents Departing, Country of Intended Stay and Purpose of Journey 1978

Country of Intended Stay	Visiting Relatives	%	Holiday Accompanying Business Traveller	%	Attending Convention, Business Employment	%	Other and Not Stated	%	Total	%
AFRICA	3,226	33.4	3,958	41.0	1,757	18.2	709	7.4	9,650	100.0
AMERICA:										
Canada	3,630		4,517		1,616		936		10,697	
U.S.A.	10,090		64,763		25,713		7,521		108,086	
Other	2,023		3,405		728		666		6,823	
Total America	15,743	12.5	72,683	57.9	28,057	22.3	9,122	7.3	125,605	100.0
ASIA:										
Hong Kong	2,769		28,522		6,924		2,014		40,230	
India	1,755		4,614		1,307		840		8,517	
Indonesia	1,235		25,757		4,132		1,786		32,911	
Japan	577		7,416		6,276		917		15,185	
Malaysia	3,557		10,755		4,335		1,215		19,862	
Philippines	1,364		10,032		4,051		1,213		16,660	
Singapore	2,109		25,921		8,562		2,088		38,679	
Thailand	529		6,633		1,419		613		9,194	
Other & unspecified	6,649		18,352		5,765		3,179		33,943	
Total Asia	20,545	9.5	138,000	64.1	42,771	19.9	13,866	6.4	215,181	100.0

Continued/..........

Table 166. / Continued ......

Country of Intended Stay	Visiting Relatives	%	Holiday Accompanying Business Traveller	%	Attending Convention, Business Employment	%	Other and Not Stated	%	Total	%
EUROPE:										
France	1,386		3,708		1,659		754		7,506	
Germany (b)	6,427		5,136		3,172		1,272		16,007	
Greece	8,712		19,820		884		1,945		31,361	
Italy	16,347		13,451		2,569		2,314		34,681	
Netherlands	6,360		3,890		830		572		11,653	
Switzerland	954		1,575		1,336		262		4,127	
U.K. & Ireland (b)	56,750		105,977		17,952		9,162		189,839	
Yugoslavia	6,265		8,327		2,974		932		15,655	
Other & unspecified	9,819		16,416				1,685		30,765	
Total Europe	113,020	33.1	178,299	52.2	31,377	9.2	18,897	5.5	341,594	100.0
OCEANIA:										
Fiji	1,639		51,920		5,501		2,569		61,629	
New Caledonia	299		13,797		1,139		2,032		17,267	
New Zealand	39,968		132,480		24,612		12,674		209,735	
Papua New Guinea	4,655		7,984		9,081		3,096		24,817	
Other	1,231		21,407		3,571		1,648		27,857	
Total Oceania	47,793	14.0	227,588	66.7	43,905	12.9	22,019	6.4	341,304	100.0
Not Stated	3,659	12.7	17,490	60.5	4,702	16.3	3,049	10.5	28,901	100.0
Total	203,987	19.2	638,019	60.1	152,568	14.4	67,661		1,062,234	100.0

205

CHAPTER EIGHT
SUPPLY OF ACCOMMODATION

As the world travel market has expanded, so has the supply and availability of tourist accommodation. In this chapter, I shall be examining the use and availability of registered accommodation in countries throughout the world.

Two main problems exist in any discussion about tourist accommodation; firstly, the question of definition, and secondly of splitting the accommodation users by type. Most of the figures that are published on world accommodation refer to the number of bedspaces, i.e. the number of beds in "hotels and similar establishments", this being the standard definition used by the World Tourism Organisation. By "similar establishments", they mean inns, motels and boarding houses, and the definition excludes such facilities as youth hostels, recreation centres for children, holiday centres, camping sites — where we would speak of places rather than beds — mountain chalets, convalescent homes, sanatoria (health being a legitimate reason for a tourist visit), rented rooms, apartments and houses, and others.

AVAILABILITY AND USE OF SUPPLEMENTARY ACCOMMODATION

The problem is that figures on these supplementary accommodation facilities are very patchy, and although both the O.E.C.D. and the W.T.O. do give figures, there are inevitably ommissions which only confuse the issue; certainly they make the findings incompatible.

The best figures are on Europe, and show that these types of supplementary accommodation are extremely important. An analysis of the use of all types of accommodation by type shows that supplementary accommodation accounts for the following proportions of total accommodation: (1979 figures)

Austria	39.0%
Belgium	37.5%
Bulgaria	34.0%
Cyprus	13.0%
Czechoslovakia	36.0%
Denmark	49.0%
Finland	36.0%
Germany, East	29.0%
Germany, West	30.0%
Greece	7.0%
Hungary	63.0%
Italy	35.0%

Table 167.   The Availability of Tourist Accommodation

(1,000 beds)	Year	Hotels	Boarding Houses	Inns	Motels	Youth Hostels	Recreation Centres for Children	Holiday Centres
Austria	1980	———— 635.3 ————				11.8	26.5	
Belgium	1979	———— 88.6 ————				(2)	28.8	39.7
Bulgaria	1979	102.9			(1)			
Cyprus	1979	7.8						
Czechoslovakia	1979	67.3		14.0	(1)			25.2
Denmark	1980	———— 68.6 ————				8.7		
Eire	1979	41.2	—— 5.9 ——			2.2		
Finland	1980	42.0	——15.0——		3.7	6.7		
France	1979	913.1			(1)	14.0		171.5
Germany East (GDR)	1979	———— 70.5 ————				22.3		
Germany West (FDR)	1980	568.0	234.9	239.7	(1)	67.3	21.0	
Greece	1979	251.0	3.9	8.6	2.1	2.0		6.5
Hungary	1979	———— 32.8 ————						
Italy	1979	1,140.0	256.4	143.7	(1)	9.1	(3)	(3)
Luxembourg	1979	14.8				1.4		
Malta	1979	10.0	——— 2.9 ———					
Netherlands	1979	88.0	12.9	—— (1) ——		6.1	— 1,394.3 —	
Norway	1980	45.4		46.3	4.3	7.4		
Poland	1979	50.9	—— 42.5 ——		(1)	44.1		517.6
Portugal	1980	58.4	37.3	3.4	0.8	——— 9.0 ———		
Romania	1979	135.7		69.4	(1)	102.3		
Spain	1980	596.9	217.5	168.8				
Sweden	1980	61.3	—— 36.1 ——		17.4	11.3		25.3
Switzerland	1980	———— 269.2 ————			6.5	8.7	(3)	
Turkey	1980	36.4	1.6	1.3	10.0			5.6
United Kingdom	1978	867.0	507.0	—— (1) ——		20.5		
Yugoslavia	1980	246.1	5.3	12.0	9.4	56.0		98.5

Continued/..........

Table 167./Continued........

(1,000 beds)	Year	Camping Sites/Places	Mountain Chalets	Sanatoria and Convalescent Homes	Rented Rooms, Apartments and Houses	Others	Total
Austria	1980	0.5	7.5	15.7	414.8	74.6	1,186.7
Belgium	1979	298.2		3.1			458.4
Bulgaria	1979	11.4	25.1		148.4		287.8
Cyprus	1979		1.3		0.8		9.9
Czechoslovakia	1979	13.9	20.7	33.8		13.8	188.7
Denmark	1980	0.5					77.8
Eire	1979	4.2				7.7	61.2
Finland	1980	761.1			1,600.2		2,428.7
France	1979	1,886.8				62.9	3,048.3
Germany East (GDR)	1979	374.9					467.7
Germany West (FDR)	1980	1.3		112.8	751.2	106.3	2,102.5
Greece	1979	44.2			83.1		401.4
Hungary	1979	46.1			120.7	33.4	233.0
Italy	1979	837.1	(3)	(3)	1,840.5	257.2	4,484.0
Luxembourg	1979	41.4					57.6
Malta	1979				22.0		34.9
Netherlands	1979					2.1	1,503.4
Norway	1980	240.4					343.8
Poland	1979	137.6	4.3	15.3	114.0	22.9	949.2
Portugal	1980	179.2					288.1
Romania	1979	57.8			37.9		403.1
Spain	1980	272.8				1,053.5	2,309.5
Sweden	1980	234.4	1.3		65.5		452.6
Switzerland	1980	260.7	(3)	6.1	360.0	187.0	1,098.2
Turkey	1980	0.4		0.3	0.6		56.2
United Kingdom	1978	1,345.0			355.0		3,094.5
Yugoslavia	1980	291.5	7.5	11.6	298.5	13.6	1,050.0

Source: OECD / World Tourism Statistics / Own Estimates
Notes: (1) Included in hotels (2) Included in holiday centres (3) Included in others

Table 168. Use of Tourist Accommodation 1979

% breakdown	Hotels	Motels	Boarding Houses and Inns	Camping Sites	Rented Rooms, Villas and Flats	Youth Hostels	Others	Total
Austria	——	61.4	——	5.5	27.4	0.7	5.0	100.0
Belgium	——	62.5	——	22.9	6.4	— 8.2	—	100.0
Bulgaria	—	65.8	—	.	19.4	14.2	.	0.6	100.0
Cyprus	86.5	.	0.3	.	13.2	.	.	100.0
Czechoslovakia	59.1	2.1	1.0	17.9	-	-	19.9	100.0
Denmark	——	51.3	——	44.9	-	3.8	-	100.0
Finland	— 59.7 —		3.6	——36.7——				100.0
Germany East (GDR)	58.2	1.2	11.6	19.1	-	9.9	-	100.0
Germany West (FDR)	55.6	-	13.6	13.4	11.0	2.5	3.9	100.0
Greece	— 89.4 —		3.1	6.0	-	-	1.5	100.0
Hungary	36.6	-	-	18.7	36.1	-	8.6	100.0
Italy	— 53.0 —		12.0	14.8	17.9	0.4	1.9	100.0
Luxembourg	— 37.5 —		5.4	51.4	-	5.7	-	100.0
Malta	Holiday Villages: 42.9%			Rented Rooms etc. 57.1%				100.0
Netherlands	— 56.0 —		2.3	32.4	-	5.5	3.8	100.0
Norway	43.7	-	17.7	33.6	-	5.0	-	100.0
Poland	53.4	0.9	10.5	11.6	7.8	0.5	15.3	100.0
Portugal	74.0	1.3	9.7	14.5	-	-	0.5	100.0
Romania	— 89.6 —		.	6.9	-	0.2	3.3	100.0
Spain	——— 95.0 ———			5.0	-	-	-	100.0
Sweden	37.1	7.3	3.7	33.2	9.7	3.0	6.0	100.0
Switzerland	55.1	1.2	-	7.6	27.0	1.4	7.7	100.0
Turkey	74.6	6.6	0.9	4.7	-	-	13.2	100.0
Yugoslavia	56.9	1.2	0.9	23.6	14.4	0.8	2.2	100.0

Source: OECD / World Tourism Statistics / Own Estimates

Luxembourg	63.5%
Netherlands	42.0%
Norway	38.0%
Poland	35.0%
Portugal	15.0%
Romania	10.0%
Spain	5.0%
Sweden	52.0%
Switzerland	44.0%
Turkey	19.0%
Yugoslavia	41.0%

We can see from the above breakdown that supplementary accommodation is of considerable importance in a number of countries, and in fact is more important than hotels and similar establishments in Hungary (high use of rented dwellings), Luxembourg (mainly due to camp sites) and Sweden (again due to camp sites). Overall supplementary accommodation probably accounts for one-third of accommodation usage in Europe.

If we note that the proportional importance of supplementary accommodation lowers in the more southerly countries, and in more tourist-orientated countries such as Spain, Portugal, Cyprus and Greece (under 10% in all these), we can assume that supplementary accommodation will be less important in most other world regions with the exception perhaps of North America. Regions such as South America, Oceania, Africa, and the Far East are undoubtedly likely to house most of their tourists — certainly over 90% — in hotels. But it is important to remember these exclusions when considering the total accommodation market.

USERSHIP OF ACCOMMODATION FACILITIES BY SOURCE

Some figures have been produced on the users of hotels, i.e. whether they are nationals or foreigners. In Chapter Six, I reproduced Horwath & Horwath figures which showed that foreign visitors accounted for 54% of total hotel consumption worldwide in 1980, against 65% in 1978. However, this is much higher in most world regions, and lowered mainly by tourist usership of hotels in North America, where only 20% of hotel users in U.S.A. and 24% in Canada are foreign.

In the other regions, the proportion of hotel business accounted for by foreigners is much higher.

Again taking Europe as an example, some figures are available on the use of tourist accommodation by nationals and foreign visitors. These refer to all types of accommodation, and therefore provide a balance with the Horwath & Horwath figures which only cover major hotels.

The proportion of hotel business accounted for by foreign (overseas) visitors 1980 is as follows:-

Total	54%
Africa	84%
Asia	74%
Oceania	38%
Caribbean	69%
Central America	92%
Europe	47%
Far East	85%
Middle East	74%
Canada	24%
South America	37%
Mexico	47%
U.S.A.	20%

Source: Horwath & Horwath International
Note: Rounded figures

Table 169.   Use of Tourist Accommodation in Europe: Proportion of Users that are Foreign 1979

Austria	75%
Belgium	27%
Denmark	44%
Finland	26%
Germany, West	9%
Italy	31%
Norway	33%
Portugal	44%
Sweden	22%
Switzerland	45%
Turkey	30%

Source: Various, mainly OECD

AVAILABILITY OF HOTEL ACCOMMODATION

There are, according to my calculations, 17 million beds available in hotels and similar establishments around the world. Almost half of these are in Western Europe, and a further one-third in North & Central America.

Table 170.   Number of Bedplaces in World: Regional Breakdown

	1976	1977	1978	1979	1980
Western Europe	7,625	7,747	7,828	7,988	8,090
Eastern Europe	938	985	1,020	1,029	1,040
North and Central America	4,616	4,681	5,062	5,132	5,251
South America	776	821	868	889	901
North Africa and Middle East	302	317	324	335	347
Africa	108	121	135	147	156
Far East	393	427	447	476	491
Oceania	469	484	505	517	530
Other	150	165	175	190	200
Total	15,377	15,748	16,364	16,703	17,006
% Change	-	+ 2.4%	+ 3.9%	+ 2.1%	+ 1.8%

The sum total of 17 million bedplaces worldwide in 1980 more or less concurs with the estimates made by the World Tourism Organisation in 1976 and 1977, although these were in fact slightly higher. They estimated that there were 16.3 million beds in hotels in 1977, against my figure of 15.7 million.

Unlike the WTO, the main growth year according to my figures was 1978 when a 4% increase in bedplaces added 616,000 beds to the total available. By 1980, the growth had slowed to under 2%.

The WTO survey from which the figures below were taken indicated the role of accommodation facilities as being not merely a basic condition of tourist development but should be regarded "in a much broader context as they make an important contribution to the economy as a whole, by stimulating economic development, social contacts and commercial activities." Certainly with business a prime motive for overseas travel, the provision of good hotel facilities can encourage conference visitors and the business market in general, and most third world countries interested in developing tourism as an industry include sizeable programmes for the construction of new accommodation facilities in their development plans.

Table 171. Distribution of Hotel Bed-places in the World

Region	Number of Countries	Available Bed-places in Hotels and Similar Establishments (thousands)		% Change 1977/1976	Change in Absolute Figures (thousands)
		1976	1977		
Africa	37	239.0	263.0	10.0	24.0
Americas	32	5,955.2	6,160.0	3.4	204.8
East Asia and Pacific	17	840.6	872.0	3.7	31.4
Europe	32	8,632.6	8,791.3	1.8	158.7
Middle East	8	113.9	124.4	9.2	10.5
South Asia	7	104.1	113.4	8.9	9.3
Total	133	15,885.3	16,324.0	2.8	438.7

Comparative costs of accommodation can have a marked effect on the popularity of a particular country, and they are often used in promotions. Two examples below show comparative costs for two examples of tourist accommodation in European countries.

Table 172.   Comparative Costs of Accommodation 1980

Cost of a single hotel room including bath and breakfast for one night (luxury)	
	$ Dollars
Austria	79
Belgium	111
Denmark	46
Eire	85
Finland	78
France	106
Germany, West	88
Greece	116
Italy	107
Netherlands	89
Norway	80
Portugal	59
Spain	44
Sweden	114
Switzerland	97
United Kingdom	125

Source: Confederation of British Industry: "West European Living Costs 1981"

Table 173.   Comparative Costs of Accommodation 1980

Cost of a double room in a 3-star hotel	
	$ Dollars
Austria	51
Belgium	43
Denmark	54
Finland	47
France	59
Germany, West	54
Netherlands	41
Norway	70
Sweden	64
Switzerland	68
United Kingdom	70

Source: Finnish Tourist Board

MAJOR HOTEL GROUPS

The WTO also concluded that a significant proportion of new accommodation supply will be contributed by hotel chain operators, including airlines, and in fact about 15% of the world's available bedspaces are contributed by the 20 leading hotel chains. These are dominated by the Americans, who account for the largest five in terms of number of rooms. Holiday Inns and Best Western are well on top by this criteria; Holiday Inns have a 2.5% world market share. The leading European hotel chain is Trusthouse Forte in the United Kingdom.

Franchising will undoubtedly be a major aspect of hotel development, which is expected to become increasingly diversified. The WTO concluded with three other broad trends:-

— more budget accommodation due to mass market travel;

— more sport and recreational facilities in hotels and construction;

— falls in staffing levels, increases in building/operation costs.

Table 174. The 20 Leading Hotel Chains in 1980

	Country	Number of Hotels	Number of Rooms
1. Holiday Inns	U.S.A.	1,755	303,578
2. Best Western	U.S.A.	2,761	207,299
3. Sheraton	U.S.A.	418	107,966
4. Ramada	U.S.A.	635	94,000
5. Friendship Inns	U.S.A.	1,080	78,500
6. Trusthouse Forte	U.K.	810	72,299
7. Hilton Corp.	U.S.A.	203	71,804
8. Federation Nationale	France	4,345	71,711
9. Supranational	Switzerland	370	70,000
10. Howard Johnson	U.S.A.	521(e)	59,000(e)
11. Golden Tulip	Netherlands	350	55,000
12. Balkantourist	Bulgaria	684	51,443
13. Flag Inns	Australia	652(e)	50,000(e)
14. Days Inns	U.S.A.	315	44,000
15. SRS Hotels	West Germany	159	43,900
16. Quality Inns	U.S.A.	350	41,415
17. HRI	U.S.A.	145	40,000
18. Club Med	France	132	36,333
19. Novotel	France	283	35,214
20. Hyatt Corp.	U.S.A.	58	34,000

Source: Service World International (including SWI estimates)

HOTEL OCCUPANCY

According to figures published by Pannell Kerr Forster (see Bibliography), the world hotel occupancy level is 73%, i.e. 73% of the total number of bedspaces available are filled. Regionally, this is higher in North America than Central America, and lower in the Middle East than in other Third World countries. It is particularly good in the Far East area, and fairly average in Europe.

Table 175. Hotel Occupancy Rates 1979, 1980

	1979	1980
World	74.7%	73.2%
Canada	72.4%	81.8%
Mexico	88.6%	86.6%
Central America	74.2%	66.7%
Caribbean	72.1%	70.6%
South America	77.1%	74.8%
Europe	74.1%	70.2%
Africa	76.9%	78.5%
Middle East	71.1%	69.6%
South East Asia	76.8%	82.0%
South Asia	73.2%	70.2%
Far East	80.5%	79.3%
Oceania	76.9%	76.7%

Source: Pannell Kerr Forster, quoted in "Catering & Hotelkeeper"

REGIONAL STRUCTURE OF HOTEL ACCOMMODATION

Using our standard eight regions, we can now look in more detail at the availability of hotel accommodation within these broad groups, recalling again that the figures refer to hotels, motels, inns and boarding houses and beds therein.

Western Europe accounts for 50% of the total world accommodation facilities. Three countries have over 1 million beds — France, West Germany and Italy — while Spain is just short of this total. France and Spain each account for about 20% of total bed facilities, well ahead of the United Kingdom which has under 10% of the European total.

The countries of **Eastern Europe** contribute just over 1 million beds to the world total — about 6%; three countries in Western Europe have greater hotel facilities than all the Eastern bloc combined, including the U.S.S.R. with under 100,000 hotel beds. Holiday-orientated countries such as Yugoslavia and Romania contribute the largest proportion of the total, 27% and 20% respectively.

North and Central America is the second main area of hotel accommodation, with over 30% of the world total. Three-quarters of this is in the U.S.A., 12% in Canada and

8% in Mexico, leaving only 3% in the Caribbean and other parts of the region.

Under 1 million bedspaces are available in **South America**, and 40% of these are in Brazil, 25% in Argentina.

North Africa and Middle East contribute a meagre 350,000 bedplaces to the world total. Despite this fairly low total, this region has the lowest occupancy level of all the ones covered in the Pannell Kerr Forster Survey.

Under 1% of the world's available hotel bedspaces are in **Africa**, and the total in the **Far East** is also fairly low at under half a million. 25% of these are to be found in Japan. A similar number of beds are to be found in **Oceania**, almost 50% in Australia, and 20% in Hawaii.

To summarise, the ten largest countries in the world in terms of bedplaces in hotels are:-

	'000 Beds	% of Total World
1. U.S.A.	4,000	24
2. France	1,632	9
3. Italy	1,573	9
4. West Germany	1,043	6
5. Spain	983	6
6. United Kingdom	735	4
7. Canada	680	4
8. Austria	667	4
9. Mexico	397	2
10. Brazil	368	2
Others	-	30
Total	-	100

Source: Own Calculations

Table 176. HOTEL ACCOMMODATION

Region 1 : Western Europe

'000 Beds	1975	1976	1977	1978	1979	1980
Andorra	2	2	2	2	2	2
Austria	606	625	638	656	666	667
Belgium	97	96	96	92	89	91
Cyprus	4	5	5	6	8	9
Denmark	55	57	61	64	69	69
Finland	49	50	51	54	57	61
France	1,672	1,681	1,668	1,574	1,600	1,632
Germany, West	961	979	999	1,020	1,033	1,043
Gibraltar	2	2	2	3	3	3
Greece	185	213	231	246	266	257
Iceland	2	2	3	3	3	3
Ireland	46	46	40	41	47	47
Italy	1,494	1,507	1,519	1,535	1,550	1,573
Jersey	20	20	20	25	25	25
Liechtenstein	1	1	2	2	2	2
Luxembourg	14	14	14	15	15	15
Malta	9	10	12	12	13	15
Monaco	3	4	4	4	5	5
Netherlands	104	107	109	106	109	110
Norway	81	84	88	95	95	96
Portugal	91	96	100	100	116	119
San Marino	1	1	1	1	2	2
Spain	972	975	976	976	977	983
Sweden	103	105	105	107	111	115
Switzerland	277	276	275	274	271	276
Turkey	124	127	130	130	135	135
United Kingdom	650	662	677	692	719	735
TOTAL	7,625	7,747	7,828	7,835	7,988	8,090

Source: WTO/OECD/National Offices/Own Estimates.

Table 177.   HOTEL ACCOMMODATION

Region 2 : Eastern Europe

'000 Beds	1975	1976	1977	1978	1979	1980
Albania	-	-	-	-	-	-
Bulgaria	99	100	102	104	103	104
Czechoslovakia	133	154	166	170	172	172
East Germany	62	65	66	70	70	70
Hungary	29	29	31	32	33	34
Poland	78	80	82	90	93	94
Romania	194	195	200	201	206	205
USSR	65	70	80	85	88	88
Yugoslavia	239	245	258	268	264	273
TOTAL	899	938	985	1,020	1,029	1,040

Source: WTO/OECD/National Offices/Own Estimates.

Table 178.   HOTEL ACCOMMODATION

Region 3 : North & Central America

'000 Beds	1975	1976	1977	1978	1979	1980
Antigua	3	3	3	3	4	4
Aruba	3	3	4	5	4	5
Bahamas	32	32	33	33	33	35
Barbados	6	7	8	10	10	11
Belize	1	1	2	2	2	2
Bermuda	9	10	13	13	14	14
Bonaire	-	-	-	-	-	-
British Virgin Isles	-	1	1	1	1	1
Canada	669	670	670	675	675	680
Costa Rica	3	4	4	5	5	6
Cuba	-	1	1	1	2	2
Grenada	2	2	3	3	3	4
Guadeloupe	3	3	4	4	4	4
Guatemala	8	9	10	10	12	13
Haiti	4	5	5	5	5	5
Honduras	5	5	5	5	5	5
Jamaica	16	17	17	18	18	20
Martinique	3	3	4	4	4	4
Mexico	355	360	365	380	395	397
Montserrat	-	-	-	-	-	-
Netherlands Antilles	7	8	9	9	10	10
Nicaragua	1	1	1	1	1	1
Panama	9	9	6	9	10	10
Puerto Rico	9	8	8	9	8	10
St. Kitts	-	-	-	1	1	1
St. Vincent	-	-	1	1	1	1
Trinidad & Tobago	4	4	4	5	5	6
U.S.A.	3,250	3,450	3,500	3,850	3,900	4,000
TOTAL	4,402	4,616	4,681	5,062	5,132	5,251

Source: WTO/OECD/National Offices/Own Estimates.

Table 179.   HOTEL ACCOMMODATION

Region 4 : South America

'000 Beds	1975	1976	1977	1978	1979	1980
Argentina	220	223	227	229	229	232
Bolivia	11	11	12	13	14	14
Brazil	279	301	325	353	366	368
Colombia	39	43	47	48	50	50
Chile	22	25	26	28	28	29
Dominican Republic	6	6	7	7	7	8
Ecuador	22	24	28	30	34	36
Guyana	-	-	-	1	1	1
Paraguay	3	3	4	6	6	6
Peru	48	49	52	53	53	54
Suriname	-	-	-	-	-	-
Uruguay	20	23	23	25	23	25
Venezuela	65	68	70	75	78	78
TOTAL	735	776	821	868	889	901

Source: WTO/OECD/National Offices/Own Estimates.

Table 180.   **HOTEL ACCOMMODATION**

Region 5 : North Africa & Middle East

'000 Beds	1975	1976	1977	1978	1979	1980
Algeria	14	15	16	17	16	17
Bahrain	12	12	14	15	15	16
Iran	19	21	21	23	22	23
Iraq	5	8	10	10	10	9
Israel	50	51	54	55	55	57
Jordan	25	27	28	30	31	32
Kuwait	4	4	5	5	6	7
Lebanon	6	6	7	7	7	7
Libya	8	9	9	9	9	9
Morocco	43	45	42	35	38	42
Oman	-	-	-	-	1	1
Qatar	5	5	6	6	7	7
Saudi Arabia	15	16	18	18	20	20
Syria	20	20	21	21	23	23
Tunisia	63	61	64	70	72	74
United Arab Emirates	-	-	-	-	-	-
Yemen	2	2	2	3	3	3
Yemen, South	-	-	-	-	-	-
TOTAL	291	302	317	324	335	347

Source: WTO/OECD/National Offices/Own Estimates.

Table 181.   HOTEL ACCOMMODATION

Region 6 : Africa

'000 Beds	1975	1976	1977	1978	1979	1980
Angola	4	4	5	5	5	5
Benin	1	1	1	1	1	1
Botswana	-	-	-	-	1	1
Burundi	-	-	-	-	-	-
Cameroon	5	6	6	7	7	8
Central African Republic	-	-	-	-	-	-
Chad	-	-	-	-	-	-
Comoros	-	-	-	-	-	-
Congo	-	1	1	2	2	2
Egypt	17	18	20	24	24	26
Ethiopia	-	-	-	-	1	1
Gambia	2	2	2	2	3	3
Ghana	2	2	3	3	3	3
Ivory Coast	8	9	9	10	10	11
Kenya	15	17	18	20	22	22
Lesotho	-	-	-	-	-	-
Liberia	-	-	-	-	-	1
Madagascar	1	1	1	2	2	3
Malawi	1	1	2	2	2	3
Mali	1	1	1	2	2	2
Mauritius	3	3	4	4	5	5
Mozambique	3	3	3	3	4	4
Namibia	1	1	1	1	2	2
Niger	-	-	-	-	1	1
Nigeria	4	4	5	6	6	7
Senegal	5	5	6	6	6	6
Seychelles	1	2	2	2	3	3
South Africa	7	7	8	8	10	10
Sudan	-	-	1	1	1	1
Swaziland	2	2	2	2	2	2
Tanzania	7	6	6	7	8	8
Togo	2	2	2	2	2	2
Uganda	1	1	1	1	1	1
Upper Volta	1	1	2	2	2	2
Zaire	4	5	5	6	5	6
Zambia	3	3	4	4	4	4
TOTAL	101	108	121	135	147	156

Source: WTO/OECD/National Offices/Own Estimates.

Table 182.　　　　　　　　HOTEL ACCOMMODATION

Region 7 : Far East

'000 Beds	1975	1976	1977	1978	1979	1980
Afghanistan	8	8	9	9	9	9
Bangladesh	7	7	8	8	8	8
Bhutan	-	-	-	-	-	-
Brunei	-	-	-	-	-	-
Burma	-	-	-	-	-	-
China	-	-	-	-	-	-
Guam	1	1	1	2	2	2
Hong Kong	24	24	26	27	28	28
India	30	32	35	35	36	36
Indonesia	25	26	29	30	32	34
Japan	114	118	120	123	133	137
Korea, South	21	24	28	30	36	39
Laos	-	-	-	-	-	-
Macau	4	4	5	5	5	6
Malaysia	23	25	30	31	32	33
Maldives	-	-	-	-	-	-
Mongolia	-	-	1	1	1	1
Nepal	2	3	3	5	5	5
Pakistan	18	18	24	24	29	29
Philippines	25	30	32	35	34	36
Samoa	-	-	-	-	-	-
Singapore	20	21	21	23	24	24
Sri Lanka	9	11	10	12	13	13
Taiwan	10	13	15	14	15	17
Thailand	26	28	30	33	34	34
TOTAL	367	393	427	447	476	491

Source: WTO/OECD/National Offices/Own Estimates.

Table 183.   HOTEL ACCOMMODATION

Region 8 : Oceania

'000 Beds	1975	1976	1977	1978	1979	1980
Australia	186	195	202	210	215	224
Cook Islands	-	-	-	-	-	-
Fiji	145	148	150	155	156	158
French Polynesia	4	4	5	5	5	5
Hawaii	85	90	95	100	100	101
New Caledonia	2	2	2	2	2	3
New Zealand	24	26	26	26	32	32
Papua New Guinea	2	3	3	4	4	4
Solomon Islands	-	-	-	-	-	-
Tonga	-	-	-	1	1	1
Vanuatu	1	1	1	2	2	2
Western Samoa	-	-	-	-	-	-
TOTAL	449	469	484	505	517	530

Source: WTO/OECD/National Offices/Own Estimates.

CHAPTER NINE
PROMOTION OF TOURISM

So far in this book, we have looked at the numbers of people travelling to the countries and regions of the world; how much they spend; what form of travel they use, and why they travel. But travel is not merely a business/leisure activity, it is also the basis for a considerable world industry which depends, directly or indirectly, on the international travel market. In this section, I want to look at some of the ways in which tourism is promoted by the main types of tourist concerns.

In every country in the world that actively encourages tourism (which are basically the countries covered in this book) there is a national tourist board; there may be more than one covering selected sectors within the tourist industry. One of the main roles of the national tourist board is to actively encourage tourists to come to the country. And they also generally publish statistical information on the country concerned.

The role of the tourist board is a broad one, and it encompasses the development of the country's tourist demand as a whole, rather than any vested interests within it. And it may be called upon to restore the image of a country which may have been affected by adverse international publicity; following the change of power in Jamaica, the Jamaican tourist board was given the task of restoring a tourist market hit by natural disaster, political uncertainty and violence, which it has attempted to do by promotion overseas.

The interests of the tourist boards may conflict with other concerns within the tourist industry. In Mexico, the tourist board has been very critical of the high prices charged in hotels within the country; they are concerned with the prospective development of the country's tourist position in the world market.

National tourist boards promote their country's market by advertising overseas, and obtaining publicity in the travel press. Various other publicity ploys are used; in 1980, the Finnish Tourist Board published a cost comparison survey for Western Europe featuring comparative costs for various types of tourist services — no guesses for the country which came out best.

The second main group of concerns to promote tourism are the major airlines, although their interests are more specific. They are, of course, keen to promote tourism to countries where they hold major routes, but they generally view the competition from other airlines as being a greater threat than the competition from other countries where they have few routes.

Promotional efforts by airlines thus generally concentrate on the services they provide, cost advantages, ease of booking and so forth; reasons why they might be chosen in preference to another airline. They are not concerned why people travel to countries, as long as they travel by air; advertising campaigns by British Airways often feature people visiting friends and relatives, which is of little interest to say, the hotel industry.

Car rental firms are also keen to promote their services rather than the countries in which they have most impact. This is mainly because the large companies have offices in most countries and at most airports, so they are less prone to fluctuations in demand between countries. Similarly **travellers' cheques** and **credit card** companies have an international market, and tend to promote their services rather than tourism in general.

Concerns within the **hotel industry**, are, of course, affected by fluctuations in tourism demand, and also the extent of the usage of registered accommodation. Their interest in international tourist demand is dependent on the extent to which they rely on overseas visitors, and the numbers of foreign tourists who use hotels. As we have noted, the proportion of foreign visitors in major world hotels was, on average, 54% in 1980 according to Horwath & Horwath; but in Africa, it was 84%, and the U.S.A. only 20%.

Also most hotels rely on other concerns in the trade, such as tour operators and travel agents for their bookings, so their direct interest in the overseas tourist is limited. With so many variables, there is little effort by most hotel groups to promote tourism to countries in which their hotels are located.

The following table shows the amount of money spent by some of the above concerns in advertising during 1979, and provides a comparison with some other major industries including automotives and tobacco. The figures cover the main countries of Western Europe, and refer to press advertising.

So we have noted that it is only really the national tourist board who is concerned with the promotion of tourism as such, financed and aided by the government itself. But in addition, the **travel operators** themselves have, of course, a keen interest in international tourist flows.

A neat distinction exists between the interests of the national tourist office, and hence the government, and the travel agents and tour operators. In the case of the former, it is tourist intake which is of paramount importance, bringing foreign currency into the country, into the shops, hotels and restaurants. In the case of the latter, they are concerned with the numbers of people travelling abroad, who will in effect be spending the currency of the country overseas. So in other words, the travel operators' gain is the government's loss. The airlines, financial concerns and car rental concerns may gain either way; but the accommodation industry will, like the government, only benefit from tourist consumption.

Organised travel, or package tours as they have come to be known, have been a major growth area in the international tourism market. They are of course primarily

Table 184.   Advertising Expenditure on Travel in Europe 1980

U.S. $000's		International	Austria	Belgium and Luxembourg	Switzerland	Federal Republic of Germany	Denmark	Spain	France
Airlines	Aug 79	13,930	806	1,337	2,635	14,881	1,026	999	7,255
	Sept 79	14,185	715	1,213	2,784	13,218	945	908	6,973
Alcoholic drinks	Aug 79	5,994	542	3,743	6,718	75,093	3,502	3,285	11,484
	Sept 79	5,832	671	3,637	6,393	71,361	3,355	2,969	11,290
Car rental	Aug 79	1,194	98	286	131	3,622	38	179	1,380
	Sept 79	1,131	78	263	126	3,460	46	158	1,482
Corporate	Aug 79	4,202	494	255	270	8,038	216	170	1,751
	Sept 79	5,013	447	199	295	7,970	219	106	2,243
International banking	Aug 79	10,947	414	202	665	5,767	317	310	2,263
	Sept 79	10,792	351	149	671	4,662	264	232	2,076
Motor cars	Aug 79	5,994	5,723	18,096	20,157	78,652	3,081	1,753	17,116
	Sept 79	5,882	6,416	17,720	21,323	82,402	2,999	1,639	17,890
National tourist offices	Aug 79	475	312	633	860	4,321	497	149	1,309
	Sept 79	485	337	606	978	4,200	450	154	1,338
Smoking materials	Aug 79	6,930	381	4,573	15,088	62,759	2,684	568	4,855
	Sept 79	6,977	384	4,405	15,601	62,587	2,538	594	4,775

Continued/..............

Table 184./Continued..........

U.S. $000's		Great Britain	Italy	Ireland	Norway	Netherlands	Sweden	Finland	Total	Change
Airlines	Aug 79	11,400	5,773	*	422	2,979	1,220	422	65,085	
	Sept 79	11,169	5,217	*	413	2,770	1,142	448	62,064	-3,021
Alcoholic drinks	Aug 79	22,809	28,792	*	23	8,055	1,930	95	172,875	
	Sept 79	21,649	28,501	*	24	8,233	1,759	142	165,816	-7,059
Car rental	Aug 79	1,773	458	*	53	477	103	151	9,943	
	Sept 79	1,471	462	*	54	456	80	147	9,414	- 529
Corporate	Aug 79	8,533	2,366	*	107	831	320	243	28,196	
	Sept 79	8,456	2,423	*	102	815	332	263	28,883	+ 687
International banking	Aug 79	9,181	949	*	94	770	224	156	32,259	
	Sept 79	8,991	1,008	*	95	877	221	150	30,539	- 1,720
Motor cars	Aug 79	47,419	33,746	*	2,356	17,771	5,277	2,155	259,296	
	Sept 79	49,243	32,952	*	2,304	19,359	4,929	2,356	267,414	+ 8,118
National tourist offices	Aug 79	6,264	920	*	108	1,196	653	168	17,865	
	Sept 79	6,363	907	*	112	1,171	541	167	17,809	- 56
Smoking materials	Aug 79	32,790	1,942	*	—	8,828	2,396	179	143,973	
	Sept 79	33,774	2,147	*	—	9,313	2,423	167	145,685	+ 1,712

Source: Campaign Europe, January 1980
Note: * Figures for Ireland were unobtainable due to a postal strike

veered towards holiday travel, but over recent years, they have become of mounting importance in the business and conference market.

In 1980, 80% of bookings in major hotels were advance reservations; and a third of these were through tour operators and travel agents. This refers to all bookings, whether from within the country or overseas.

Table 185. Worldwide Reservations Through Travel Agents and Tour Operators 1976-80

(% of advance bookings)	%	All Advance Bookings
1976	34.7	81.2
1977	30.5	80.6
1978	32.3	80.8
1979	28.5	79.3
1980	27.7	80.0

Source: Horwarth & Horwarth

Table 186. Advance Bookings by World Region 1980

	All Advanced Bookings	Of which: Thru' Tour Operators and Travel Agents
All	80.0	27.7
Africa	83.4	45.1
Asia	72.7	31.3
Australasia	96.7	24.7
Caribbean	83.9	41.6
Central America	60.0	33.0
Europe	83.7	23.8
Far East	77.4	35.8
Pacific Islands	95.3	41.5
Middle East	71.6	17.9
Canada	80.3	24.1
Mexico	63.3	43.7
U.S.A.	76.8	15.5
South America	87.2	14.5

Source: Horwath & Horwath

This refers to all bookings at major hotels, and in the following table, I have estimated the proportion of overseas tourist visits which are advanced bookings, and those which are through travel operators. According to these estimates, 90% of hotel reservations are advanced bookings, and 40% are via travel operators.

Table 187. Estimated Proportion of Advanced Bookings by Overseas Tourists 1980

	% Advanced Bookings	Of which: Through Travel Operators (%)
All	90	40
Africa	97	65
Asia	86	50
Australasia	99	28
Caribbean	95	52
Central America	80	65
Europe	92	32
Far East	88	54
Pacific	99	47
Middle East	84	28
Canada	90	34
Mexico	70	75
U.S.A.	83	24
South America	95	20

Source: Own Estimates

But holidays or business trips involving stays at hotels are more likely to involve a travel operator, and the overall proportion of tourist trips using organised travel operators will be lower than this suggests. In fact, usage of organised travel firms varies considerably between countries. Around 40% of tourist trips by UK residents to other countries are organised, and organised trips account for over 50% of all holiday visits. But the West Germans prefer to organise their own trips; in 1980, only around 15% of their tourist trips were organised. Much depends, of course, on geographical location, and the character of the population, but the role of the operators themselves is also a central one, and their promotional efforts are vital to the industry.

The advantages for the organised travel operators is that, like the airlines, they can switch direction if there is a marked change in tourist flow. A good example of this was the tremendous promotion of the U.S.A. as a tourist destination in 1980, following the air fare price war and the weakness of the dollar. Tour operators in many European countries focussed their advertising on package tours to the States; Marilyn Monroe said "Some Like it Hot — Miami" on posters; French travel agents showed a collage of U.S. souvenirs ("the real thing is better"); in Sweden, A Swedish Red Indian (sic) dreamed of Disneyworld. The operators can, in effect, research their market and veer their promotional efforts accordingly.

1980 does not seem to have been a very good year all round for the tour operators and travel agents. This has partly been due to the slackening in demand on the international tourist scene, although as we have seen, this did not actually amount to a fall in demand. So perhaps the problems in the travel industry have been more due to a decrease in the number of tourists using organised travel services. The 1970's have undoubtedly been the heyday of the package tour, and the 1980's may see more tourists planning their own trips.

Looking at one important area in 1980 — Northern Europe — there were distinct downturns in demand for package holidays from Scandinavia (- 30% over 1979), Benelux (- 10%) and West Germany (- 15%); only the United Kingdom saw a rise in that year (+ 5-10%).

1981 has apparently been a better year, although no firm figures are yet available.

As yet, I have made no distinction between tour operators and travel agents, but they are, of course, different. Travel agents merely provide the facility for booking tourist trips, including package tours, but also airline seats and other travel bookings. The tour operators are more directly linked to the package tour industry, but both mainly depend on organised travel. Only the big travel agents advertise; mainly it is the tour operators themselves, with most of the promotion focussed on the holiday market. And generally, the destination takes second-place to the cost, image and service which the operator wishes to convey; only if there is a distinct growth in the popularity of a specific destination will travel operators focus the attention of their advertising upon it.

In theory, the travel agents are in a better position to take advantage of fluctuations in demand than the tour operators, who are directly involved in package tours, and have to set up the arrangements for transport and accommodation. But in practice, there has been a decrease in the use of travel agencies in many countries with more direct tourist bookings. And both suffer if the demand for organised travel falls.

To summarise, many types of concerns involved in the tourist industry actively promote tourism in general, but they all have vested interests, and only the national tourist boards make the destination itself their primary concern. The majority of advertising, by airlines, finance companies, car rental firms and travel operators sell their own services more than the popularity of travel — they assume that the demand is there, and if it is not, they can look for it elsewhere. So it is down to the governments, not to **private** enterprises to actively promote tourism as a concept in itself.

The Growth in World Travel 1975 - 1985
(1975 = 100)

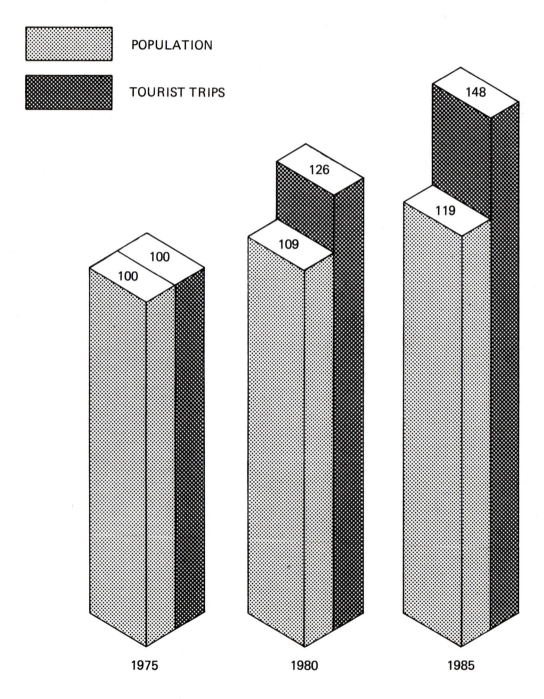

POPULATION

TOURIST TRIPS

100 100

109 126

119 148

1975   1980   1985

CHAPTER TEN
FUTURE OF WORLD TRAVEL

The world travel market is set to continue to expand over the next decade, although perhaps not at the same rate as in the 1970's.

The total number of persons taking trips in the world is expected to rise to 418 million by 1985, which will be around 9% of the total world population. In terms of regional flows, Western Europe will continue to dominate for some time to come, although its overall market share will show a slight fall. Travel to countries in Eastern Europe and South America is expected to show only a slight increase, and the main growth areas are forecast to be Africa, the Far East and Oceania. By 1985, the Far East is expected to take a 6.2% market share compared with 4.7% in 1980, while Oceania's share will rise from 1.7% in 1980 to 2.3% by 1985.

The market for tourism was worth around $121.5 billion worldwide in 1981. It is expected to continue to increase during the first half of the 1980's at a rate of around 16% per annum, reaching $218 billion by 1985. The share of the market held by Western Europe will fall to just over 50%, with a further 25% held by North and Central America.

Table 188.   Projected Total Number of World Tourist Trips 1981-1985

(millions)	Total World Population	Tourist Trips	%
1981	4,500	365	8.1
1982	4,575	378	8.3
1983	4,650	390	8.4
1984	4,750	408	8.6
1985	4,825	418	8.7

Table 189. Projected Value of World Tourism Receipts to 1985

($ billion)	1981	1983	1985
Western Europe	66.0	85.0	109.0
Eastern Europe	3.5	4.2	5.0
North and Central America	26.0	36.0	55.0
South America	2.3	2.8	3.5
North Africa and Middle East	6.0	7.5	9.5
Africa	2.7	4.0	6.0
Far East	9.0	12.0	17.5
Oceania	6.0	8.5	12.5
Total	121.5	160.0	218.0

Source: Own Estimates

Table 190. Analysis of World Tourism Demand to 1985

(millions)	1981	1983	1985
Western Europe	222.0	235.0	250.0
Eastern Europe	46.0	48.0	50.0
North and Central America	50.0	54.0	58.0
South America	7.3	7.5	7.7
North Africa and Middle East	9.8	10.0	10.3
Africa	5.5	6.2	7.0
Far East	18.0	21.5	26.0
Oceania	6.8	8.0	9.5
Total	365.4	390.0	418.5

Source: Own Estimates

APPENDICES

Compiling international comparative statistical data on any subject is a hazardous business, not least in the field of tourism. The problems are obvious; each country in the world has its own way of collecting and presenting information; some do so more regularly than others; and the information they collect will differ. Yet national sources are both the most detailed, and the best, place to go to find out about the tourism of a particular country.

I hope that in this book, I have provided a grounding of information on world travel trends, but clearly it has not been possible to examine any particular country in detail. It is probable that readers of this book will seek to obtain more information on particular aspects, and particular countries, and I would like to summarise the sources used in this book, and the methods by which additional material may be obtained.

Two international organisations publish tourism statistics on countries throughout the world. The **World Tourism Organisation**, which is an arm of the United Nations, publishes several studies containing statistical information on countries throughout the world. Its most detailed volume is the "Yearbook of Tourism Statistics" which, on a country-by-country basis, presents figures on tourist arrivals, length of stay, nights spent and so forth. The WTO data is based on information sent to them by national statistical and tourist offices, so there is an inevitable time-lag; the next edition, which should be published in Spring/Summer 1982, will contain information (in most cases) for 1979 and 1980. The WTO does however publish various digests with more up-to-date, if more basic and less complete information, within them.

The other main organisation is the Organisation for Economic Co-operation and Development (OECD), which publishes **"Tourism Policy and International Tourism"** every 12 months. This only covers OECD member countries, which is most of Western Europe bar the smaller countries, Canada, the U.S.A., Japan, Australia and New Zealand. The OECD publication also draws on national sources, but throws in some estimates of its own, and being only concerned with more developed countries, is more up-to-date in its presentation; the next edition should be published in October, 1982 and will contain 1981 figures.

Both these organisations make considerable efforts to compile international travel statistics, but despite their extensive research facilities, there is little effort to reconcile figures which are clearly not comparable. While this is not a problem with their own publications (where such inconsistencies are clearly stated) there is a tendency for private research organisations to extract WTO and OECD data and lump it all together as being a guide to world trends. In this book, this course has been carefully avoided; I have sought by the free use of estimates to present comparative data in order to provide a more realistic survey of world patterns than some that may have gone before.

Various other private organisations publish useful studies on particular aspects of world tourism, which are reasonably priced and generally available annually.

"**The Big Picture**" published by Asta Travel News, New York, is a survey of world travel trends with particular emphasis on North American markets and U.S. travellers abroad. It is an extremely useful publication with a wealth of information, and at $38 dollars per issue, well worth subscribing to. The '81/'82 edition has just been published containing figures up to 1980 and some general pointers for 1981.

Two publications feature information on hotel use and occupancy; "**Trends in the Hotel Industry**" by Pannell, Kerr Forster, and "**Worldwide Lodging Survey**" by Horwath & Horwath, both U.S. publications. In addition, a magazine called "**Service World International**" lists the top hotels in the world.

Statistics on world air transport are available in another annual publication, by the International Civil Aviation Authority entitled "**Civil Aviation Statistics of the World**". The 1981 edition with 1980 figures is currently available, containing fairly comprehensive figures on passengers carried internationally by country and major airline.

"**World Air Transport Statistics**" contains more detailed information on the major airlines, most of which are members of the International Air Transport Association (AITA). The next edition will be available in Autumn, 1982 and contain 1981 figures.

The best international source for tourism receipts and expenditure is the "**Balance of Payments**" bulletin published by the International Monetary Fund, which gives figures on travel credits and debits, and fare receipts and payments. The figures are reasonably up-to-date (1980 has been out for a while) but they are presented in "SDRs" and have to be converted at the given exchange rate. Also, the figures often do not tally with national sources.

In addition to these main international studies, the best course of action for further research is to contact the national statistical offices and tourist boards within the countries concerned. Write to their addresses within the country; state precisely the information you require, and allow at least six weeks for a reply from a developed country and 10 weeks for a developing country. This is the only way to obtain detailed information on a particular country, and they will reply, sending information free or at little cost.

World Tourism Organisation,
Capitan Haya, 42
Madrid-20
Spain

Tourism Policy and International Tourism,
Director of Information OECD,
2 rue Andre-Pascal,
75775 Paris Cedex 16,
France

The Big Picture,
Asta Travel News,
488 Madison Avenue,
New York NY 10022,
U.S.A.

Trends in the Hotel Industry,
Pannell Kerr Forster,
420 Lexington Avenue,
New York, NY 10170,
U.S.A.

Service World International,
205 East 42nd Street, Rm 1815,
New York NY 10017,
U.S.A.

Worldwide Lodging Survey,
Horwath & Horwath International,
919 Third Avenue,
New York NY 10022,
U.S.A.

Civil Aviation Statistics of the World
  International Civial Aviation Authority,
PO Box 400, Place de l'Aviation Internationale,
10000 Sherbrooke Street West,
Montreal, Quebec,
Canada H3A 2R2

World Air Transport Statistics,
International Air Transport Association,
26 Chemin de Joinville,
PO Box 160,
Cointrin Geneva,
Switzerland

National Tourist Offices in many countries

National Statistical Offices in many countries

Balance of Payments,
International Monetary Fund,
Washington DC 20431,
U.S.A.

Campaign Europe

Wall Street Journal

Travel Trade Gazette - Europa

Travel News

Business Traveller

The Times

Financial Times

Financial Weekly

Investors Chronicle

The Economist

Confederation of British Industry

United Nations   — Yearbook of National Accounts Statistics
                — Statistical Yearbook
                — UN Monthly Bulletin

Euromonitor   — European Marketing Data and Statistics
               — International Marketing Data and Statistics

The World Bank

World of Information

The terms adopted in this study are based on the definitions used by the World Tourism Organisaton:

A TOURIST is a temporary visitor staying in a country for at least 24 hours for one of the following reasons:-

— leisure (recreation, holiday, health, study, religion, sport)
— business
— family
— conference
— mission.

EXCURSIONISTS are people not staying 24 hours in the country. They are excluded from this study as far as possible, which is completely for the developed countries, and in the majority of cases in developed countries. However, in the less developed countries, the statistical information on tourist visits is not as complete and some total visitor figures (i.e. tourists and excursionists) may have been included.

Students, cruise visitors and persons in transit have been excluded, but the note above applies here also.

The WTO definitions have been adopted by most international bodies, including the OECD, who also present extensive statistics on tourism and travel.

APPENDIX IV
REGIONAL BREAKDOWNS

Region 1 : Western Europe

Andorra, Austria, Belgium, Cyprus, Denmark, Finland, France, Germany (West), Gibraltar, Greece, Iceland, Italy, Jersey, Liechtenstein, Luxembourg, Malta, Monaco, Netherlands, Norway, Portugal, San Marino, Spain, Sweden, Switzerland, Turkey, United Kingdom.

Region 2 : Eastern Europe

Albania, Bulgaria, Czechoslovakia, Germany (East), Hungary, Poland, Romania, USSR, Yugoslavia.

Region 3 : North & Central America

Antigua, Aruba, Bahamas, Barbados, Belize, Bermuda, Bonaire, British Virgin Isles, Canada, Cayman Isles, Costa Rica, Cuba, Curacao, Dominican Republic, Grenada, Guadeloupe, Guatemala, Haiti, Honduras, Jamaica, Martinique, Mexico, Montserrat, Netherland Antilles, Nicaragua, Panama, Puerto Rico, St. Kitts, St. Vincent, Trinidad & Tobago, USA.

Region 4 : South America

Argentina, Bolivia, Brazil, Colombia, Chile, Dominican Republic, Ecuador, Guyana, Paraguay, Peru, Suriname, Uruguay, Venezuela.

Region 5 : North Africa & Middle East

Algeria, Bahrain, Iran, Iraq, Israel, Jordan, Kuwait, Lebanon, Libya, Morocco, Oman, Qatar, Saudi Arabia, Syria, Tunisia, UAR, Yemen (Republic), Yemen (DEM).

Region 6 : Africa

Angola, Benin, Botswana, Burundi, Cameroon, Central African Republic, Chad, Comoros, Congo, Egypt, Ethiopia, Gambia, Ghana, Ivory Coast, Kenya, Lesotho, Liberia, Madagascar, Malawi, Mali, Mauritius, Mozambique, Namibia, Niger, Nigeria, Senegal, Seychelles, South Africa, Sudan, Swaziland, Tanzania, Togo, Uganda, Upper Volta, Zaire, Zambia.

Region 7 : Far East

Afghanistan, Bangladesh, Bhutan, Brunei, Burma, China, Guam, Hong Kong, India, Indonesia, Japan, Korea (South), Laos, Macau, Malaysia, Maldives, Mongolia, Nepal, Pakistan, Philippines, Samoa, Singapore, Sri Lanka, Taiwan, Thailand.

Region 8 : Oceania

Australia, Cook Islands, Fiji, French Polynesia, Hawaii, New Caledonia, New Zealand, Papua New Guinea, Solomon Islands, Tongo, Vanuatu, Western Samoa.